Work Placements – A Survival Guide for Students

Christine Fanthome

palgrave
macmillan

First published 2004 by
PALGRAVE MACMILLAN
Houndmills, Basingstoke, Hampshire RG21 6XS and
175 Fifth Avenue, New York, N.Y. 10010
Companies and representatives throughout the world

PALGRAVE MACMILLAN is the global academic imprint of the Palgrave Macmillan division of St. Martin's Press, LLC and of Palgrave Macmillan Ltd. Macmillan® is a registered trademark in the United States, United Kingdom and other countries. Palgrave is a registered trademark in the European Union and other countries.

ISBN-10: 1-4039-3434-7   paperback
ISBN-13: 978-14039-3434-5 paperback

This book is printed on paper suitable for recycling and made from fully managed and sustained forest sources.

A catalogue record for this book is available from the British Library.

10 9 8 7 6 5 4 3 2
13 12 11 10 09 08 07

Printed and bound in Great Britain by
4edge Ltd, Hockley. www.4edge.co.uk

Work Placements
A Survival Guide for
Students

Palgrave Study Guides

Authoring a PhD
Career Skills
Critical Thinking Skills
e-Learning Skills
Effective Communication for
  Arts and Humanities Students
Effective Communication for
  Science and Technology
The Exam Skills Handbook
The Foundations of Research
The Good Supervisor
How to Manage your Arts, Humanities and
  Social Science Degree
How to Manage your Distance and
  Open Learning Course
How to Manage your Postgraduate Course
How to Manage your Science and
  Technology Degree
How to Study Foreign Languages
How to Write Better Essays
IT Skills for Successful Study
Making Sense of Statistics
The Mature Student's Guide to Writing (2nd edn)
The Palgrave Student Planner
The Postgraduate Research Handbook
  Presentation Skills for Students

The Principles of Writing in Psychology
Professional Writing
Research Using IT
Skills for Success
The Student Life Handbook
The Student's Guide to Writing (2nd edn)
The Study Abroad Handbook
The Study Skills Handbook (2nd edn)
Study Skills for Speakers of English as
  a Second Language
Studying the Built Environment
Studying Economics
Studying History (2nd edn)
Studying Law
Studying Mathematics and its Applications
Studying Modern Drama (2nd edn)
Studying Physics
Studying Programming
Studying Psychology
Teaching Study Skills and Supporting Learning
Work Placements – A Survival Guide for Students
Writing for Nursing and Midwifrey Students
Write it Right
Writing for Engineers (3rd edn)

Palgrave Study Guides: Literature

General Editors: John Peck and Martin Coyle

How to Begin Studying English Literature
  (3rd edn)
How to Study a Jane Austen Novel (2nd edn)
How to Study a Charles Dickens Novel
How to Study Chaucer (2nd edn)
How to Study an E. M. Forster Novel
How to Study James Joyce
How to Study Linguistics (2nd edn)

How to Study Modern Poetry
How to Study a Novel (2nd edn)
How to Study a Poet
How to Study a Renaissance Play
How to Study Romantic Poetry (2nd edn)
How to Study a Shakespeare Play (2nd edn)
How to Study Television
Practical Criticism

For Alexei, Ivan and Tatiana Kalveks;
Jasmine and Daniel Fletcher;
Henry Liew and Patrick Farmbrough –
may your work placements be useful,
stimulating and good fun!

Contents

Preface

As competition for graduate employment opportunities grows, the advantages of undertaking a work placement before leaving university are becoming increasingly apparent. Forming an important bridge between learning and earning, work placements enable students to develop and practise skills, experience workplace culture, identify or confirm their career objectives and aspirations, and define and implement their own contribution. The inclusion of workplace experience on the CV indicates that the student has some practical understanding of work-related issues in addition to theoretical knowledge, and it may also demonstrate a commitment to a specific sector or profession. Unsurprisingly, employers tend to respond very positively to students who have workplace experience, which is viewed by many as the first rung on the career ladder.

This book is an essential guide for students contemplating or embarking upon work placements. Drawing upon and punctuated by comments from students, employers and tutors, it presents what is effectively a chronological account of the process of finding, securing and learning from a work placement, and includes advice and information at each stage. The idea for the book stemmed from my own experiences as Work Placement Tutor in the Humanities and Cultural Studies Department at the University of Surrey Roehampton in 2002–3, during which time it became apparent to me that students would benefit from some written guidelines as to how to tackle each step of the process and how best to approach any related assignments.

The book begins by rationalising the increase in the number of work placement opportunities, accounting for the value of work placements for both students and employers, and identifying different types of work experience. Chapter 2 focuses on how to get started and is particularly relevant for students who are as yet undecided about their career aspirations. It encourages students to reflect on what they want, not only in terms of the sector and work involved, but also with regard to factors such as location, timescale and environment. This chapter also explains how to make an audit of skills and personal attributes which may then be used in applications for work placement. It also indicates where vacancies and potential opportunities may be found. Chapter 3 contains practical advice on writing a CV and a letter of application, and emphasises the importance of keeping a record of applications made, of taking time to do background research and of maintaining a positive attitude. This is developed in Chapter 4 which focuses on how to perform well at interview. It emphasises the importance of good preparation and the benefits of thinking in advance about interview protocol and the questions that are likely to be asked. Developing the theme of self-reflection introduced earlier, this chapter also highlights the value in analysing interview performance and identifying strengths and weaknesses with a view to improving technique on future occasions. It also includes a checklist of points to confirm prior to accepting a work placement.

Chapters 5, 6 and 7 analyse the placement experience. Chapter 5 looks at how students may derive the greatest benefit from the placement in terms of developing skills and self-awareness and making contacts for the future. Chapter 6 focuses on common problems facing students and offers suggestions on how to avoid them together with remedial strategies. Many problems arise from misconceptions or a straightforward mismatch of expectations between employers and students, and with this in mind, Chapter 7 analyses the employer's perspective, outlining key concerns and explaining the rationale underpinning the employer's point of view. This chapter also examines the role of the work placement tutor and identifies how students may derive the greatest benefit from the skill and experience of their tutor. Chapters 8 and 9 comprise case studies of students encompassing a spectrum of experiences arising as a result of different types of placement in a variety of sectors. The timescale involved also varies, and includes two weeks of continuous work, one day per week for several months, six-week internships and one-year sandwich placements.

Many universities now formally assess their work placement students by means of written or oral assignments, and Chapter 10 offers guidelines on how to approach keeping a learning log, writing a reflective essay, giving a presentation and writing a report, as these are common forms of assessment. Even if these assignments are not compulsory, students are advised to give some thought to the learning outcomes associated with these tasks, as they may be key to securing a job after graduation. As a continuation of this theme, the final chapter of the book offers advice on how to embark successfully upon the career ladder after university. Drawing on the lessons learnt from all stages of the work placement experience, it identifies how to create and implement a jobsearch strategy that is likely to lead to a successful and fulfilling outcome.

Learning through experience is invaluable, and students can benefit enormously by evaluating and acting on the views of others who have already undertaken work placements. With this in mind, I have included direct quotations from interviewees at the end of most of the chapters. These relate to the areas covered within each relevant chapter and together represent a variety of perspectives on each situation which I hope will be of interest to readers.

This project would not have been possible without assistance and support from a number of sources and I should like to take this opportunity to record my appreciation. Many thanks to all the organisations who have shared resources and information, particularly the National Council for Work Experience, Bournemouth University, Brunel University, the University of Greenwich, the University of Surrey Roehampton and Dr Challoner's High School, Buckinghamshire. Special thanks are due to Ann Bennett, Karen Collier, Sue Dooks, Karen Ephram, Nicola MacLeod, Doug Perkins, Liz Rhodes MBE and Seema Shoor, and to my colleagues at Roehampton Surrey, namely Dr Anita Biressi, Chris Bond, Professor Lyndie Brimstone and Carol Prior. I am very grateful to my publisher, Suzannah Burywood, for her faith in the project in the early stages when it was expressed in just two sides of A4 paper, and to David Gibson and my husband Rudolph Kalveks for their invaluable advice and help in getting the project off the ground. Finally, and most important of all, many thanks to all the students, employers and tutors who took the time and trouble to share their opinions on all the various aspects of the work placement process covered in this book.

1 Why Do a Work Placement?

This chapter will:

- ► look at the recent expansion of work placements
- ► analyse the value of work placements
- ► identify different types of placement

► Expansion of work placements

Over recent years work placements have become increasingly visible in the curricula of universities, colleges and schools. This development has promoted a parallel expansion in supportive literature and web-based resources available to students. It is now widely recognised not only that placements are beneficial, but that, as competition for jobs intensifies, work experience is becoming an essential component of an applicant's CV within the post-graduation employment market.

The National Council for Work Experience estimates that in any one year approximately 100,000 higher education students will undertake work experience of some sort. In addition, around 550,000 Key Stage 4 pupils spend at least two weeks on work placement each year. Of the funding for education business links via Local Learning and Skills Councils from the DfES, a contribution of around £10 million is allocated to provide support for work placements for those at school. Further evidence of the growing importance of work experience may be seen in the development of foundation degrees that focus on workplace learning tailored to suit employers' specific needs. These vocationally focused degrees provide students with the experience and skills necessary to contribute immediately within a workplace environment. Foundation degrees were launched in 2001, and by September 2004 the number of places available rose to 24,000.

Liz Rhodes, Director of the National Council for Work Experience, notes that in recent years the debate about work experience has gathered momentum. She attributes this both to ongoing criticism from employers that students are leaving university with little understanding of the world of work, and also to the fact that as more and more students are encouraged to attend university, the argument being that they will have better career prospects on graduation, students themselves have the expectation of swiftly entering and contributing to the workforce. She is clear that work experience is part of the transition process from 'learning to earning' and that it is essential in today's competitive market:

> Work experience now has a crucial role to play in giving young people an intro-
> duction to the world of work. They have to understand what it is that employers
> want, and that's something that you don't necessarily get taught or made aware
> of whether you are at school, further or higher education. So there's a need to
> make people aware of the relevance of it, because the fact of the matter is,
> increasingly, if you can't show on your CV some kind of work experience, you
> are not going to get past first base. Work experience is here to stay. There is no
> doubt about that.[1]

Ivan Lewis MP, Minister for Young People, affirms that work placements make an important contribution in the overall strategy to introduce and develop relevant skills in workplace environments:

> The Skills Strategy we published in July 2003 calls on employers to get to grips
> with the fundamental importance of skills to their business – so that their staff
> have the skills and knowledge to meet current business needs and put them in
> a stronger position to develop and deliver higher value-added products and
> services. Work experience and work placements are a vital part of this.[2]

Liz Rhodes believes that the debate is ongoing and that it will remain significant and relevant, not least because, in addition to the current practice of recording the destinations of students after graduation, in the future universities are likely to be assessed on the employability of their departing students in terms of the length of time it takes them to find work. This, she asserts, will further highlight the importance of work placements, and will, in turn, impact on the skills required by work experience tutors:

> I'm trying to make out the case that in fact this whole business of preparing
> students for the world of work is actually becoming more and more important,

---

[1] Liz Rhodes, interview with author, 6 October 2003.
[2] email from Ivan Lewis's office to author, 21 October 2003.

and therefore the professional status of those individuals who are involved ought to be taken more seriously because one of the things people like that have to be able to do is to face both ways and to understand the language on both sides.[3]

In today's world, traditional learning practices are increasingly being supplemented by practical and vocational initiatives with the aim of supporting current initiatives such as those of increasing employability and widening participation. Work placements play an important role in this ongoing cultural shift and are therefore likely to achieve even greater prominence in the future.

▶ The value of work placements

In attempting to quantify the usefulness and importance of work placements it is clear that there are multiple layers to the benefits that may be derived from the experience. This chapter adopts the premise that the 'value' from the students' perspective derives from three overlapping reasons: it notes that some skills may be learnt or developed from the actual experience of the workplace; that the student's own personality may develop as a direct result of the experience; and that the work placement may be beneficial in informing and influencing career decisions.

What you can learn in the workplace

Ideally, a work placement will give you the opportunity to learn new skills and to reinforce those you already possess. Some skills are practical in nature and stem from familiarity with particular equipment, for example, mastering specific computer software packages, or the use of a telephone switchboard facility, fax, photocopier or specialised machinery. You may also get the chance to hone and develop skills you already have through constant practice, such as by researching new areas, writing reports, or spending time on your telephone technique. The placement may also act as a useful bridge between theory and practice in that it provides an arena in which you may observe and test out what you have learnt at university and thus apply your theoretical learning to a practical situation.

For many students, a work placement represents the first real opportunity to deal with issues that go hand in hand with holding down a job. At a very basic level, this may include being punctual and always arriving for work suitably presented. It may involve living on a budget, sorting out your travel arrangements and organising the rest of your life to fit in with your work. In the course of the day, you will be able to test out your time management,

---

[3] Liz Rhodes, interview with author, 6 October 2003.

self-management and organisational skills and you will see how well you are able to cope with all aspects of the job, particularly those you do not like. In summary, you will be able to analyse how well you cope with the general constraints imposed by working life. You will find out which aspects you find irksome and you will discover the aspects of the job to which you can adapt easily.

Perhaps the most useful element of placement experience is the insight it gives into workplace culture, and the opportunities it offers in terms of finding out how well individuals are able to integrate into different environments. (This will be covered more fully in Chapter 5.) Learning how to cope in the workplace is a very complex endeavour, and may determine the level of fulfilment and satisfaction that is achieved overall. Interpersonal skills are likely to be put to the test in interacting with colleagues, working as part of a team and in dealing with office politics. You will need to effect a balance between being willing to help and ensuring that you are not coerced into undertaking work with which you are not comfortable. This may be particularly relevant if you are working for more than one person, when subtle assertiveness techniques might well be required. Integrating into the workplace calls for an ability to appraise the situation and personalities involved and to present and conduct yourself in a way that is acceptable both to you and to others.

Work placements are in many ways a transition from learning to earning environments and a stepping-stone to permanent work. Not only do they bolster the CV with relevant experience, they also enable the student to test out and gain greater insight of a specific industry or profession, to watch others in a particular career role and to learn additional skills from those around them. To an extent, these experiences are common to all working environments, but what differentiates workplace experience from the type of work commonly done by students who primarily wish to earn extra money during the course of their time at university is that during a work placement it is assumed that the student will spend time observing and thinking about the experience. It is, therefore, acceptable for the student to ask questions and request and expect guidance when required. Moreover, most important of all, the work placement provides an environment within which it is safe to make mistakes. The entire endeavour has an experimental air, making it possible for the student to take calculated risks in order to achieve more. The main aim is not to master all aspects of one particular job, but to learn about workplace culture, career options and choices and how best to improve your own contribution and performance.

What you can learn about yourself
Although the practical and cultural skills that can be acquired in the workplace are very important, arguably an even more valuable aspect of work

placement experience is the opportunity it offers for reflective development and analysis. In the course of the work placement, students can reflect upon how well they coped with office culture and politics; what they enjoyed; what they found boring and problematic and where their particular skills lay. Not only does this make future choices easier, it also means that the student can hone the technique of critical reflection that is fundamental to developing the skill of organising one's own learning and personal development planning. Clearly this is a skill that underpins university study generally, and, as I shall indicate, it is essential to have grasped this in order to undertake the reflective written assignments that now accompany many courses. In an ideal situation, the work placement will provoke greater self-knowledge and self-understanding, which in turn will mean that students are then more aware of how to evaluate and improve their own personal performance, without necessarily being reliant on guidance from others.

Just as learning new skills can lead to a boost in confidence, so can finding out more about yourself and using that knowledge to make the best of the present and to plan for the future. If you are focused on and aware of your own personal development planning, you are essentially much more in control of your future. In contemporary society, the notion of 'lifelong learning' has superseded the view that education ends after school or university. By considering self-learning as an essential ongoing goal, you are equipping yourself well for your future working life, in whatever field you choose.

Career decisions and how a placement can lead to work

In an increasingly competitive marketplace, even well-qualified students may face difficulties in stepping onto the first rung of the career ladder if they do not have practical experience. Work placement schemes provide an invaluable mechanism by which this gap may be bridged. Graduates with experience can offer an employer both theoretical and proven practical experience. Just as they possess a written qualification relating to the knowledge and skills they have acquired at university, they are also able to provide references as to their attendance, competence and attitude within the workplace. These documents together mean that the potential employer is taking less of a risk in that (s)he may be reassured that the student already has a level of familiarity and experience with workplace procedures and culture. Many employers now expect graduates to have undertaken work experience in the course of their studies, and since many small businesses do not have the time or finance available to train new recruits, they actively seek potential workers who are immediately employable. Also, work experience is a way of demonstrating a student's commitment to a specific sector or job. If you undertake a work placement in your second year and then apply for similar work after you graduate, it is clear that you have been committed to your ambition for some while, that you have taken positive action to learn more about the area and that, having done that, your aims remain unchanged. This is very important, as it proves you mean what you say and shows determination and focus. Students who apply for work after graduation having shown no demonstrable evidence of interest in the area prior to that time will be at a comparative disadvantage.

Work placements may also be very important in confirming or changing previously held career plans as the actual experience may be better, worse or simply different from what was imagined. They are also an important part of career planning in the sense that if someone is interested in working in a particular industry, but is not aware of the options and jobs available, a work placement can offer valuable insight. This means that for students who only have a vague idea about what they would like to do in the future, a work placement can help in narrowing down the choices and indicating the general direction to take. Indeed, whilst in the workplace you will be able to achieve a better idea of what you want and don't want, what you are good at and what does not interest you.

You may find that you enjoy one particular aspect of the work far more than others and that you would like to spend more time focusing on that or related tasks. You may discover an aptitude for figures, writing or administration that you were only partially aware of before the work placement, and you may increasingly realise what is likely to give you the greatest job satisfaction in the long term. Equally, whilst all jobs have their own particularly tedious aspects, there may be some that you definitely do not want to contemplate as a result of your taster experience. Moreover, you may discover more about your working habits, such as whether you prefer to work alone or as part of a team and whether you enjoy working on a varied portfolio of projects or focusing primarily on one.

If you are successful in your work placement, this in itself may mean that your future application forms shine out amongst others, and the experience you gained may help you to get a better job. Also, just as whilst on placement you are likely to be networking in order to make new contacts and seek potential employers, they are also likely to be keeping an eye open for good potential employees. Similarly, people you encounter from different organisations whilst on placement may be interested in what you have to offer. You may well find that your placement acts as a 'trial period' at the end of which you have a job!

Benefits for employers

There are many proven benefits of inviting work placement students into the workplace from the employer's point of view. Not only do the students supplement the existing workforce at reasonable or no extra cost, they may also possess skills that are of direct use within the organisation, such as the ability to write reports, conduct research, give presentations or operate computer software packages. Many students may possess transferable skills, such as being able to work unsupervised and being able to solve problems, and they may be more amenable to being trained for a job in a specific way than other, more experienced workers who may be more set in their ways and used to approaching tasks from a certain perspective. Being young and relatively unused to the workplace environment may sometimes be a bonus as it means that the student may be able to view a situation with fresh eyes and offer a new solution to an old problem. Similarly, students are often able to demonstrate a level of enthusiasm that may have deserted other members of the workforce. Frequently, students are employed to deal with a particular task, possibly a backlog that would otherwise remain untouched, and as such they are able to make a valuable contribution to the organisation before moving on. The contemporary emphasis on employability and transferable skills, which has permeated many university courses, means that a great proportion of work placement students are immediately useful to employers and are able to make an instant contribution. As such their value is evident.

It may also suit employers to build closer links with local universities and colleges, especially if they are hoping to recruit graduates from those organisations in the future, and they may therefore have an incentive to become involved with a work placement programme, and take students on a regular basis. This enables employers to develop an awareness of curriculum developments, and it is even possible that long-term collaboration between work placement tutor and employer might bring to light exactly what is required in the workplace so that students can be advised accordingly and focus on the areas in question. Moreover, just as the placement offers the student the opportunity to 'test out' the workplace, it also offers the employer the opportunity to 'test out' the student. Many work placement students go on to full-time employment in the same organisation.

Work placements are highly competitive, but it is important to be aware that employers need you as much as you need them. They are not employing you in order to do you a favour – you have just as much to offer them as they have to offer you!

▶ Different types of work experience

There are many different types of work-based learning experiences, the major differences between them hingeing on the overall duration of the placement; whether it takes place part-time or in a 'block'; whether it is paid, supported by sponsorship finance, or unpaid; and the nature of any associated assessment. Work placements can be customised to suit the employer and the student, but they generally fall into one of the categories discussed below.

Sandwich courses/industrial traineeships

Sandwich courses and industrial traineeships are part of a longstanding tradition in Higher Education in the United Kingdom. Typically they take place prior to the final year of the degree and are especially prevalent in areas such as engineering and business studies. Since they are compulsory components of the degree course, there is normally ample assistance available for the student in locating and securing a placement.

Internships

Although the word 'internship' originated in the USA, it is now used in the UK and continental Europe, particularly by multinational organisations operating worldwide, for example Proctor & Gamble, Microsoft and Ernst & Young. Internships are very like industrial placements, although they tend to be for shorter periods of time, and some are offered during the summer vacation period. They are highly competitive and the closing date for applications is generally several months in advance of the placement start date. They are normally salaried, although at a lower rate than other junior positions within the workforce. Many interns go on to work for their placement organisation.

Course-specific work placements

Increasingly, more and more university departments are introducing work placement options into the courses they offer, partly in order to embrace the current initiatives for widening participation and increasing employability. The length of time on placement varies from one university to another and whilst some are done as a 'block', others are undertaken part-time over several weeks. Many course-specific work placements involve students undertaking work in a particular profession or area of industry, and there is usually help available within the university in terms of locating and securing placements. It is usually the case that there will be an obvious correlation between the subject studied at the university and the sector in which the placement will occur.

Gap year

It is now very common for students to take a gap year either before going to university or after graduation, and a large proportion use the opportunity to earn money in order to finance their studies. Work experience gained in the gap year prior to university may be influential in securing part-time work that can be undertaken in tandem with university study, thus easing the financial burden. It can also act as a useful bridge to the full-time employment market post graduation.

Vacation placements
Some organisations offer work placements in the vacations, especially if their requirements fluctuate seasonally. Vacation placements have the advantage of not interfering with university study.

Voluntary work
Voluntary work is another valid means of obtaining work experience and a great deal of choice is available as to the location and the type of work involved. Indeed, it is possible to undertake voluntary work in a huge range of areas including, for example, ecology, teaching, archaeology and local, national and international charity work. Moreover, organisations that rely on volunteers are likely to be geared towards deploying specific tasks to a variety of individuals and may be more responsive to cold calling.

International exchanges
Some students prefer to undertake work experience abroad and to take the opportunity to travel and to learn more about another country whilst on placement. There are a number of organisations that specifically arrange and support such placements (see Chapter 2).

Part-time work
Many students take on part-time work whilst they are studying, often in order to ease the financial burden. This may be seen as a form of work experience, as it provides an introduction to the workplace and ample opportunity for work-based learning.

▶ Summary

This chapter has focused on the increased presence of work placements within university course modules and school curricula and has suggested that work experience is an important bridge between theory and practice, and between learning and earning. Employers want staff who are able to make an immediate and viable contribution in the workplace, and work placements can provide the experience necessary to facilitate this. From the student's perspective, work placements assist with career choices, allow skills to be practised and developed, boost confidence and self-knowledge and represent an attractive addition on the CV. From an employer's perspective, a work placement introduces a fresh pair of eyes to the organisation, and offers a low-cost source of labour. This chapter has also listed some of the different types of work experience currently available.

Perspectives and Feedback

Well-chosen and well-managed students can provide enthusiastic, cost effective work in areas where permanent employees tend to get stuck in a groove ... I was talking to xxx recently and they had used students to search the web to find potential licensing partners for some of their technologies and they were delighted with the results: the students were clever, determined and quick.

Simon, *employer – new technology*

Work placements are extremely valuable for students on vocational degrees. Not only do they allow students to contextualise the taught part of their course but they provide valuable case study material for projects and dissertations and students develop useful contacts for their future careers. In my experience, students mature quite considerably whilst on placement and on their return, have a much broader perspective and a more grown-up attitude to their studies! In particular, when they return to start work on their dissertations, I find that they are much better at managing their time and more confident with their fieldwork. Even those students who have experienced disastrous placements do benefit – their confidence is boosted by dealing with difficult situations and they learn from reflecting on what went wrong and how they could manage similar situations in the future.

Naomi, *tutor*

The placement was organised so that I gained a wide range of skills that could be useful in almost any future career. This was useful, as I had not yet decided on what I wanted to do in the future. I found that my people skills and readiness to adapt to different situations developed significantly.

Emily, *student*

Work placements provide valuable opportunities for graduates to gain experience of the industrial sectors and complement their academic studies. Well defined schemes allow students to both apply theory to practice and learn and develop new skills.

Colin, *tutor*

Financially a placement could potentially make the difference between leaving [university] with debt and graduating with money in the bank! For [students] that may be worrying about whether or not they can afford university – this could make the difference, but should by no means be seen as a poor man's degree route.

Thomas, *student*

We get enthusiastic support on productions which are usually under a lot of pressure and it brings fresh talent and ideas to the industry.

Celia, *employer – TV production*

I was frequently surprised, and sometimes delighted, at the change which occurred when capable, but unengaged, students went on placement. The most dramatic case was a student who had performed averagely on the course with the exception of the Computer Graphics modules. She had fantastic reports on placement and when she left the course, went to work for xxx. Undoubtedly, what she learnt at college helped but there was a major breakthrough when she experienced the workplace.

Trevor, *tutor*

I gave work experience to an autistic student in our mailroom where internal mail was sorted and delivered by hand and external mail franked and collected by Post Office employees. The average age of the staff was between eighteen and twenty-five; the young man was fifteen. He was fascinated by the drinks vending machines which were on free vend and this was the breakthrough to his mixing with the other staff. He started each morning by collecting the drinks and as the days went on gradually assisted with the normal mailroom duties. By the end of his three weeks he was participating in seventy-five per cent of the work. He eventually found work in the mailroom of another company.

Delia, *employer – insurance*

The work placement was invaluable. Because I do not currently work in the sector vocational experience is as important as the academic study to build my credentials and put the course into a practical perspective.

Mark, *student*

A work placement gives an opportunity for students to see behind the scenes and the reality of day to day activity in a high profile arts organisation. It gives an opportunity to understand organisational structure and culture and may challenge preconceived ideas of the workplace as dynamic and highly creative as a lot of our work is routine maintenance and administration. For the employer, a work placement gives the opportunity to complete medium to low priority project work with extra assistance. It also offers the chance to learn from working with inexperienced individuals, particularly to gain managerial experience.

Sally, *employer – museum*

I would recommend a placement in a special school [for children with severe learning difficulties] to anyone. The experience gained there is valuable and universally applicable because, even if the teaching profession does not interest you, you gain an insight into the lives of disabled children, which will increase your social awareness and make you appreciate your own health and lifestyle far more.

Valerie, *student*

I got the opportunity to work with very talented people whose work I truly admired. I contributed a little to the creation of an exciting project – a magazine. This has always been my dream job so to get this close has now fuelled my determination to succeed! The art department were preparing for a big issue so they were busier than usual there were lots of jobs to do. It was the variety that made it interesting; I got to research in the archive, organise images, and mount up layouts. I received great contact numbers for other magazines and photo studios. I got a lot of thanks and a great reference. This will possibly open doors into a career in journalism. Also, this sort of professional placement will undoubtedly be good for my CV.

Kelly, *student*

We cannot stress enough to the students the importance of this time spent in the workplace. It is their chance to gain valuable experience and a real insight into the industry. It is also an ideal opportunity for them to build contacts with professionals. The more effort and enthusiasm the students put into the placement, the more they will ultimately gain from the experience.

Kate, *tutor*

2 Getting Started

This chapter will help you to:

- ▶ reflect on what you want in terms of your work placement
- ▶ identify what you can offer your potential employer
- ▶ think about how to find a work placement

The umbrella term 'work placement' encompasses a myriad of greatly differing experiences. The key to navigating an appropriate course through all the possibilities and identifying what most closely fits your requirements and aspirations is to ask yourself a series of questions, not just about the nature of the work you seek, but also the timescale, environment, benefits and general practicalities. This chapter will offer some guidelines on how to decide what is best for you.

▶ What do you want?

It is essential to think through what you want and what you do not want. Reflective thought will be a recurrent theme in this book, because it is fundamental not only to establishing which is the best placement for you, but also to ensuring that you get the most from the placement, that you are able to communicate what you have learnt in your tasks or assignments, and that the experience will be beneficial in terms of subsequent career decisions. Reflecting on each stage of the process may seem time-consuming, but in fact it actually guards against you wasting your time pursuing opportunities that you do not really want.

Securing a work placement is a competitive endeavour. Typically, large numbers of students chase a far smaller number of placements, and this may result in students feeling that they should be grateful for what they are offered. However, whilst flexibility on the part of the student is undeniably an advantage, it is very important not to lose sight of your primary objectives in terms of what you hope to gain from the placement. Indeed, a clear knowledge of what you want is a very valuable asset, as it will enable you to prioritise a list of potential employers and ensure that you undertake a placement that is appropriate to your aims and personal circumstances. Each student is likely to have different priorities, and aspects of each proposal are likely to be more relevant to some students than to others. Remember that your reflective thoughts are your personal property and you do not have to share them with potential employers. They are simply a mechanism for ensuring that you remain constantly aware of what you would like to achieve in the best case scenario. They represent a clear overall picture of what you want, and that is certainly a solid starting point. Moreover, they are not binding, and you may choose to compromise and negotiate.

So, whilst it is important to be as flexible as possible, as this will widen the choice of potential employers, it is nevertheless essential to be realistic about your primary aims and most particularly what is workable within the framework of your life. An awareness of any restrictions, for example in terms of timing or distance, will ensure that you do not pursue a placement opportunity that is actually not right for you. A work placement is a negotiated agreement between the student and the employer and it is important to be very clear about what you would consider to be essential, the points on which you would be prepared to compromise, and the practical arrangements that would need to be in place to enable the placement to proceed. Prior to seeking a placement, I would suggest that you make notes under three headings:

- Primary aims
- Points of compromise
- Restrictions

This exercise will not only ensure that you are absolutely clear about what you want, but later, when you consider specific opportunities within the framework of these three headings, it will also enable you to place companies in order of personal preference. There is a big difference between creating restrictions that will narrow the opportunities available and achieving an awareness of what is important to you and what is not. You can always opt to compromise, but a good starting point is a sound assessment of what would constitute the optimum placement for you, and time spent reflecting upon this prior to embarking upon the quest for a placement will reap dividends.

► Points to consider

Primary focus

If you don't have firm ideas about your future career, a work placement is useful as it will give you the chance to consider which aspects of work and working culture you find most stimulating and enjoyable, and, indeed, which aspects are potentially problematic. If you already have defined career plans, a placement experience is a good opportunity to 'test out' a particular job or industry. Some students may be interested in learning more about a specific profession, such as by investigating the work of a Press Officer or Personnel Officer, and they therefore have considerable scope in applying for a work placement as most companies of a certain size may theoretically be able to accommodate them. Alternatively, other students may primarily be interested in a product, such as television programmes or motorbikes, and may wish to gain an overall view of the industry that underpins their production whilst being flexible about the actual work they undertake during the placement. Others may wish to learn a particular new skill whilst being less concerned about the business environment. If you have an idea about your future career, it would be sensible to use your placement as a first rung on the ladder. If you are not yet sure, focus on what you are good at and what you enjoy doing. A great deal of what you will learn in the workplace is transferable and will be useful even if your final career choice is in a completely different area.

The optimum placement for an individual will be determined by her or his perspective on the aforementioned issues, and most particularly, what (s)he hopes to gain from the work placement. At this point, you may find it useful to review the various factors contributing to the value of work placements as outlined in Chapter 1, and highlight those of most significance to your own situation.

Nature of the work

As a corollary to this, it is useful if students think about whether they hope to be engaged in specific project-based tasks or whether their primary aim is to gain an overall insight into the workings of the particular office or department. Would it be beneficial if the placement were to involve periods of observation and shadowing? In terms of the actual work undertaken, how important is it to be creative/part of a team/offer support services? Are menial jobs such as filing and photocopying acceptable on the basis that these are tasks that have to be done? Are there specific tasks that you would like to try to accomplish whilst under supervision on work placement?

Environment
Is the work likely to take place inside or outside, in an office or other location? Do you thrive in an informal environment or do you prefer a more formal atmosphere in the workplace? Are you willing to adhere to the dominant dress code? Would you enjoy the experience of a large company or would you prefer to undertake your placement in a smaller organisation? Do you have definite views about working in the commercial sector or the not-for-profit sector? Do you have any special requirements that should be considered at this point, for example do you need good wheelchair access?

Timescale/availability
It is very important to identify the timescale within which the work placement will be done and to ensure that your availability coincides with your employer's requirements. Some placements call for the student to be available every day for a block of time, which typically ranges from two weeks to six months. Others are part-time in nature, requiring the student to attend on one or more days per week for a set time. Work placements may take place in term time, in the vacation, or both. Hours may be fixed or flexible and in the case of part-time placements, this may also apply to the day(s) in question. Students need to be clear about their availability and communicate this to potential employers. For example, it may be impractical to agree to a moveable day of the week for a part-time placement when lectures and university courses tend to follow a regular timetable. Similarly, since about three-quarters of students undertake part-time paid employment whilst at university in order to meet some of the associated costs, it is important that students coordinate their placement not only with the university timetable but also with any other work commitments.

Location
It is important that the journey to and from the placement is manageable and can be undertaken within a reasonable time. It is worth checking public transport links prior to pursuing a placement, particularly if unsocial hours may be involved.

Similarly, if part of the placement is to be undertaken in the vacation, it may be more realistic to opt for a location near to family or friends in order to minimise outlay on living expenses.

Finance
Some work placements are paid but many of them are not. A very small number of organisations offer sponsorship, normally awarded after a placement for the final year of study. Claims for expenses are more common and may well be met by the employer, although some organisations

have a policy of not reimbursing expenses. The situation, as outlined by the DTI, is that: 'The national minimum wage must be paid to students on work placements in the UK if they are placed from an overseas college but not from a UK college.'[4]

Does the finance constitute a problem for you? If you can only undertake a placement where travelling and subsistence expenses are met this needs to be recognised at this stage. Some universities and colleges have a fund to cover essential expenses incurred by students whilst on placement and it is advisable to explore these possibilities too. The National Council for Work Experience argues that work placements should be paid as employers reap a business benefit as a result. Liz Rhodes, Director, also notes that the contemporary emphasis on widening participation is somewhat incompatible with current work placement practices in that only fairly wealthy students can entertain the prospect of working for nothing, which means that those from non-traditional backgrounds may be at a disadvantage. However, Rhodes recognises that many employers do not have the incentive to pay as, particularly in the creative industries, there is huge competition for placements, and concludes that: 'I think the only thing one can do is to make people aware of the realities and the options and then it's up to each individual to make his own choice.'[5]

Modus operandi

Last, but by no means least, you will need to consider how you intend to identify potential organisations. Some placements are advertised, with dates and times stipulated from the outset, whilst other businesses may wait to be targeted by students or may not have considered the possibility of a work placement student until the first approach is made. Reading advertisements for work placements may be very beneficial for students who do not initially have fixed ideas about what they would like to do, or conversely, who wish to explore a particular scheme offered by a company in which they have a specific interest. However, these placements are less likely to be flexible in terms of timescale and duration, particularly for those students who are aiming to undertake a part-time placement. Many students apply for formal schemes whilst also exploring the possibilities of 'custom-made' placements in companies of their choosing. Universities differ as to the amount of support and guidance they are able to offer in terms of finding a

---

[4] email to author from DTI spokesperson, 4 December 2003. Further information on the national minimum wage may be obtained from the telephone helpline 0845 6000 678, or website reference www.dti.gov.uk/er/nmw.

[5] Liz Rhodes, interview with author, 6 October 2003.

placement. This can range from a specially appointed work placements tutor whose job it is to explore, locate and negotiate placements, support the student throughout and give advice on assignments, to a situation in which the onus is on the student. The process of finding a placement will be covered more fully shortly, but it is important at this early stage to think in general terms about what might be the best routes for you.

If you have thought reflectively about all these areas, you should now have a very clear indication of the practical considerations required to ensure that you feel comfortable in your placement. These thoughts, combined with your earlier reflections on the value of the work placement for you, and most specifically the desired outcomes, should guarantee that you are now equipped to proceed to the next stage of seeking and securing a work placement. However, these conclusions reflect only half of the story: you also need to be aware of what you can offer the organisation within which you will be working.

▶ What can you offer?

Prior to composing your CV and letter of application, it is essential that you reflect on what you are good at, what you can already do, and where you believe that your, as yet untapped, talents may lie. As you make a list of these factors, remember to bear in mind that many of your skills and a great deal of your experience may be transferable in the sense that it could be useful in the workplace even if that is not the environment in which it was acquired.

As you compile your list, try to think of yourself as a commodity. Do not exaggerate, but do not underestimate what you can do. It may be helpful mentally to break down your 'life CV' into various sections and reflect upon what you have learnt from each. Sections could include previous work experience, university experience, hobbies, your family situation, generic skills and personal attributes.

Previous work experience/transferable skills

Most students have at some time had a part-time job and, indeed, a large proportion continue to work whilst they are at university. Without elevating the status of any previous work experience, analyse the skills that you drew upon and note any evidence to support the assertion that you make a good employee. For example, if you have held down a job for some while, this may indicate that you are a reliable person who has experience of the culture of the workplace. You may also feel that your experience with fellow employees at different levels has enabled you to develop interpersonal, social and communication skills. Your job may have given you a chance to demonstrate written or oral communication skills, if, for example, it involved writing letters and emails, and dealing with telephone enquiries. You may have acquired specific skills that are of use elsewhere, such as the use of computer equipment and software packages, or you may have gained financial experience. Think about what was required of you – did the job call for punctuality, organisational skills, or time management, for instance? Would these skills be useful in another environment?

University experience/transferable skills

Do not forget the skills you have acquired in higher education. Your course work may have called for research and analysis, report writing and presentations, which may in turn have involved using computer packages such as PowerPoint. Consider how your research data were gathered – this probably involved a certain amount of empirical work combined with library skills. Moreover, you may have been required to undertake qualitative or quantitative research, and then to analyse your findings. You may have been called upon to think creatively and to suggest solutions to specific problems, and you may also have been required to assess your own progress reflectively and make the necessary adjustments. University students require an ability to focus, and most demonstrate both the ability to work in teams and to work independently during the course of their degrees. All of these skills are relevant to the wider working experience and increase employability.

Hobbies

Are you able to demonstrate an interest in a particular field through long-standing membership of a relevant association or club? Could your enthusiasm now be combined with transferable skills so that you are able to present yourself to an employer as someone who is both useful and committed? Have you held any office in connection with your hobby in the past, for example by being treasurer of a school or university club? Have you visited any sites or exhibitions in connection with this interest? Do you regularly receive and read related literature and do you have any particular ideas that you would like to develop?

Personal circumstances

Sometimes personal circumstances can be a positive advantage in that they demonstrate a person's experience and understanding of a situation. Your experience may be directly or indirectly relevant. An example of direct relevance might be, for example, a dyslexic student working for the Dyslexia Association. An example of indirect relevance might be a single parent, who, in running a household single-handedly together with coordinating the needs of the children with his or her own studies, is likely to rely upon well-honed organisational skills. Consider your own personal circumstances – do they say anything about you that might influence either the area of placement in which you might be interested or the nature and tone of your letter of application?

Generic skills

Remember that you do not have to have acquired your skills through schooling, higher education or indeed through work. They may have developed simply as a result of life experience. Ask yourself if your own lifestyle has enabled you to develop generic skills such as problem solving and the ability to work in a team. If you feel that you possess generic skills, be confident in listing them on your CV and work placement application.

Personal attributes

The same advice applies to personal attributes. If you feel that some of your personality traits and ways of dealing with situations present you in an advantageous light, then you should mention them. Personal attributes might include flexibility, adaptability, practical common sense, the ability to stay calm in a crisis and the ability to work on your own without supervision. You will notice that certain 'buzzwords' recur in advertisements and personal profiles. It is essential that you are able to use the same language as your potential employer, so ensure that you are aware of these terms and use them in your applications if they effectively convey what you wish to explain. (Terms might include 'thinking outside the box' – having original thoughts; 'interpersonal skills' – talent for dealing with people; 'holistic view' – overall comprehensive approach; 'multi-disciplinary' – covering many areas, and so on.) If you are not comfortable and conversant with these terms, it may help to make a list of them from careers literature and job advertisements, write down your own interpretation of their meanings and learn them.

Remember that the reason for reflecting on previous jobs, current and previous study skills, hobbies, and personal and lifestyle circumstances is to define what you have to offer your employer. This is likely to be a combination of 'hard' skills that you have already acquired, transferable skills, and a list of aspects of your personality that are indicators of how well you would do the job in question. You will need to persuade your work placement employer that you will be an asset to his business and that the experience will be beneficial for him as well as for you. You therefore need to focus on your potential contribution to the company and all the advantages to you joining the workforce.

▶ How to look for a work placement

Students may choose to apply for placements that are advertised and/or they may choose to develop their own ideas as to which businesses to target. The preliminary pointers outlined below offer some suggestions as to how to start.

University resources

As soon as possible, arrange a meeting with your work placement tutor, if you have one, in order to discuss the best options for you. Your tutor is likely to have a database of contacts through which you will be able to search, and in addition, (s)he may know of upcoming opportunities within the local community. Your university may also have a student employment service, Jobshop or careers advisory team to help you find a placement or at least target organisations that are likely to welcome applications. If your degree subject is relevant to the placement you hope to secure, it is likely that your departmental office may hold data that will be useful in your search, for example the names and contact numbers of alumni or former work placement students who may now be working in your chosen field. The careers advisory service will also be able to inform you of recruitment and work placement fairs.

National, local and trade press

Searching through job advertisements in national and local newspapers will give you a strong sense of what employers are looking for and which businesses are likely to be amenable to offers of help. If you feel you can offer what they are looking for, it is worth contacting the relevant organisation and enquiring about the possibility of a work placement whilst emphasising the contribution you could make. Similarly, if you know the area in which you would like to be placed, scan the companies mentioned in the relevant trade press for ideas of where to apply. The Yellow Pages or Thompson's local directories may also yield the names of potential businesses to target.

Personal contacts

Think about your own personal network. Do you have friends or acquaintances who work within your chosen field and who may either be in a position to offer you a work placement or who would be able to give you suggestions as to who you should contact? Friends' parents may be particularly useful in this respect, as they are likely to be sympathetic to the situation. You do not have to know someone well to send them a polite email or letter asking for guidance. Use your initiative to determine who might be well-placed to assist you.

Web-based resources

The Internet provides quick and easy access both to lists of work placement vacancies and also to advice and support for students considering or undertaking work placements. The best place to start is the National Council for Work Experience's site (address below), as this contains not only an extensive list of available placements but also relevant supplementary information for those seeking placements. In addition, there are also many sites that address and cater for students with specific requirements, for example, those with disabilities; those who are only considering placements in one particular region of the country or relating to a specific area of study; those from ethnic minorities and students who are interested in work placements overseas. In order to find the sites that are most relevant to you, you might try some of those listed below, or explore the additional links cited on these websites, or conduct your own web search.

www.prospects.ac.uk

This is an extremely useful website, and has links with www.work-experience.org (the National Council for Work Experience). These websites contain both lists of current work experience vacancies and also useful advice and information about the benefits of work placements and how students can get the most from them. In searching for vacancies, students can focus on specific locations, various timescales and a range of types of placement. There is also a related website that deals specifically with mini-pupillages and vacation placements within the legal sector.

www.STEP.org.uk
www.secureyoursuccess.co.uk

Secureyoursuccess is the sub-section of STEP (Shell Technology Enterprise Programme), specifically for students. It offers an undergraduate programme involving small businesses across the UK in addition to on-line support for writing a CV and producing a work placement portfolio.

www.summerjobs.com

This site focuses on summer jobs and seasonal employment.

www.gowales.co.uk

GO Wales features work placement opportunities in small businesses across Wales.

www.business-bridge.org.uk

Business Bridge is a partnership between three Liverpool based universities that aims to provide students with work experience in marketing, graphics, web design, finance, IT, engineering and languages.

www.bridgenortheast.org.uk
Based on Business Bridge, this website focuses on specific projects in the north east of England.

www.gradsouthwest.com
The Careers Advisory Service together with the University of Exeter run this jobshop service, based in the south west of England.

www.qub.ac.uk/scisho
This Science Shop introduces universities in Northern Ireland to the local science community, with the aim of putting students and staff in touch with those who are able to offer relevant work.

www.yini.org.uk
Yini.org caters mainly for students of engineering, science, computing and business, and looks at how to make the most of a year in industry. Areas covered include professional institutions and women in technology.

www.worklink.org.uk
The Young Professionals Group of the British Computer Society (www.bcs.org.uk) offer this specialist service to students seeking work placements in their gap or sandwich years.

www.internjobs.com
This is a national database of worldwide internships for students and graduates.

www.projecttrust.com
This is an organisation working in 24 developing countries. Students undertake a year's voluntary work abroad.

www.gapyear.com
This organisation locates and supports work placements in the UK and overseas.

www.AIPT.org
The Association for International Practical Training arranges assignments in the USA.

www.iaeste.org
The International Association for the Exchange of Students for Technical Expertise organises placements abroad.

www.aiesec.org
An international student organisation that arranges traineeship exchanges abroad.

www.CIEE.org
The Council on International Educational Exchange arranges hundreds of short-term projects in 32 countries overseas.

www.blackandasiangrad.co.uk
This website aims to enhance the employability of black and Asian students in the United Kingdom. It includes information on undergraduate vacancies and related events such as recruitment fairs.

www.opportunities.org.uk
Opportunities.org supports people with disabilities and assists them in finding and keeping work.

www.skill.org.uk
Skill is the National Bureau for Students with Disabilities. The website includes case studies from students with disabilities who are engaged in higher education and training. Skill has published a booklet entitled *Into Work Experience* which focuses on the positive experiences of disabled people. It includes information on the value of work placements, the Disability Discrimination Act in relation to work placements and a list of useful organisations and contacts.

▶ Summary

This chapter has highlighted the fact that work placements come in different shapes and sizes! It has shown that students need to think reflectively about their individual situations in order to decide where, when and under what circumstances they would ideally like to undertake a placement. It has emphasised the importance of defining the contribution that would be made to the business by pinpointing relevant skills and experiences. Finally, it has indicated how students may begin to make initial enquiries about how to find a work placement.

Perspectives and Feedback

Students who start their preparations early will always get the best placements. These students use all the resources available to them and don't expect to be successful straight away. It's always a good idea to build in plenty of time as inevitably there will be a few rejections before the placement is secured.

Naomi, *tutor*

It's important to work out what you want to do with your career. This sounds obvious but many placement people are unfocused and come a poor second to those who know what they want. This will determine where you look. Make a direct approach – find out the name of the appropriate person to talk to by calling potential organisations. Then email them and follow up with a call. Use directories, but also look at job ads and check out which organisations are offering the types of jobs you think you might be interested in. Always see the placement as a means to an end but don't just think about the next step – the one after that is the most important.

Annabel, *employer – PR*

I decided to go for a placement in the radio industry because I would like to have a career in the music industry when I graduate. I wanted to take this opportunity to further my knowledge and I also wanted to meet and work with people who do the job I'd be interested in.

Anastasia, *student*

At the beginning of the second year, students tend to have very set ideas about which companies they would like to work for during their placement. We try to emphasise that good experience can be found in such a wide array of companies no matter how large or small the organisation and that it is down to students and their willingness to learn to make the placement a successful one. Talking to other students who have previously been through the placement experience can be a great motivator for them and helps to broaden their horizons.

Kate, *tutor*

As a high-profile organisation in the cultural sector we are inundated with applications from highly qualified and motivated individuals.

Therefore we have the pick of the very best of applicants. We do not necessarily shortlist applicants who state: 'I have always loved beautiful objects and know I would love working with you' but would favour good practical and interpersonal skills.

Sarah, *employer – museum*

The worst problem I ever had was with two students at a drama school where they were to help backstage with students' productions. One of the students injured herself badly whilst using some kind of tool when helping to build a set. So the insurance situation needs to be investigated thoroughly before the placement starts.

Jenny, *tutor*

I submitted my CV and then had a couple of meetings with the management team. During these I made it clear how much time I could give to the placement especially regarding my commitment to my university course and paid work. Also I think it is important to determine how the individual is going to add value during their placement. Whilst the student is not looking for payment there is an argument that says they are (hopefully) contributing and should perhaps be reimbursed expenses.

Mark, *student*

Take time to identify what it is that you want to get out of YOUR placement. This may include what 'skills' should I be developing so that I will have a clear advantage in any future graduate employment market? Or how will the placement help me to get the best class of degree I can?

Derek, *tutor*

3 Applying for a Placement

This chapter will point out the importance of:

► keeping a record of your applications
► doing background research
► maintaining a good attitude

It will show you how to:

► write a CV
► compose a letter of application

► Keeping a record

Finding a work placement can be a lengthy process involving false leads, rejections and redirections on the route to eventual success, so it is important to be very organised about keeping track of any opportunities you discover and applications that you submit. The first stage is to set up a computer file or buy a notebook in which you can record your progress on the way to securing a placement. This is essential, since you are likely to be speaking on the telephone or writing to a considerable number of people, and if you are then invited for interview it is important that you are able to track the correspondence and recall the information that you have already given, together with the response to it. An alphabetical system may be best as it is quick and easy to use, and you should keep your notes in one place so that if, for example, you are telephoned unexpectedly, you will be able to retrieve them quickly and recall the background to the particular application. In your file you should note the progress of all applications, including

27

the names of anyone to whom you have spoken on the telephone, plus the relevant dates and any suggestions that were made. Retain the original advertisement and person specification, if there is one, as it is often useful to remind oneself of the basic requirements prior to attending an interview. You might also keep a copy of your covering letters. Even if you are not offered a placement at the time, this file could be very useful after graduation when you are searching for a permanent job. Moreover, reflecting on the data collected could be helpful later as, with the benefit of hindsight, you may see ways of improving your application procedure. You should indicate, for example, with an asterisk against the relevant name, if anyone has been particularly helpful as you may need to contact him or her again in the future.

It is a good idea to arrange the organisations in which you have an interest in order of priority, and to refer to your list sporadically as you embark upon new applications. Whilst it may be unrealistic to hope to contact companies individually and wait for an answer before proceeding, it is nevertheless not very practical to process too many applications simultaneously. You may find yourself in the position of being offered a placement you don't really want because you are holding out for your first or second choice. On the other hand, placements take some time to set up and it is important to know when to move on or you may run out of time. You may be applying for placements in an area in which you would like to work permanently after graduation so it is doubly important to behave professionally, as the people with whom you are corresponding now may become your colleagues in the future. One solution might be to approach two or three companies at a time in the order of your priority list, and if you get an offer, notify those higher on the list who are still deliberating prior to accepting or declining the offer in hand. It is important to be in control of the situation at all times.

▶ Background research

If you are responding to a specific advertisement for a placement, it will be clear as to what is expected and to whom you should apply. However, if you are cold calling, you may start with only the name of the company. In the first instance, find out and note down the full postal address and contact details in your placement record. Secondly, telephone the organisation and ask if they offer any work placement schemes. This may save you wasting your time in submitting a CV and letter, as at this point some organisations will inform you that they definitely do not take work placement students under any circumstances. However, unless you are refused at this point, ask for the name of the person you should contact and his/her job title, and check that you are clear about the spelling. If the switchboard operator is unable to help you, ask for the Personnel Office and try again. If you write to a specific person, you are far more likely to elicit a reply. Not only will your letter reach someone who may be in a position to help you, but the fact that you have tracked the correct person down will indicate that you have initiative and common sense.

Check that you have web details for the organisation and spend some time researching their website. It may be that one division of the company is working in an area that relates specifically to an aspect of your study or previous experience. Ensure that you know the name of the Managing Director and the Head of the Department in which you would like to be placed and that you have a broad understanding of the company's business, most important clients, products and so on. In the case of a public company, you may find it useful to request a copy of the Report and Accounts, as this will give you an up to date insight into recent successes and the current direction and objectives of the company. Read the trade press and note any news items relating to organisations you are targeting. Not only does this show you are focused and that you are up to date with your information, but it also provides a useful topic of conversation in an interview situation.

Before applying, take the time to consider how you might best contribute to the company. Think about the areas that most interest you and whether you have any previous experience or specific skills that might enhance your application. Remember that the employer is primarily motivated by what you have to offer her or his organisation. You only have one opportunity to request a work placement, so make sure that you have researched all the facts you need and that you have thought through your application before you proceed to the next stage.

▶ Attitude

Attitude is of paramount importance when applying for a placement. In the first instance, a proactive attitude is essential to secure a placement, particularly when there is often great competition for positions. In order to get a placement you will need to remain focused on your objectives and pursue your enquiries with unobtrusive determination. The background research that you have done is important here too, as it will be obvious when you talk to potential employers whether or not you have bothered to find out about the company concerned and whether or not you have really thought through what you hope to achieve from the placement. Whilst it is a good idea to seek guidance from those who are in a position to advise you, such as your university tutor, it is nevertheless essential that you use your own initiative in seeking a placement, even if eventual success comes via a recommendation from someone else. Be prepared to hand your tutor a list of areas that interest you and suggestions regarding specific companies when you meet initially to discuss your potential placement. This will give your tutor a better idea of what might suit you, and it might prompt him or her to recall appropriate contacts or other suitable companies not on your list. However, there is a fine line between appreciating the assistance you receive from your tutor and expecting her or him to find a placement on your behalf. Dependency is a negative quality and something that is likely to deter employers. It simply is not impressive to announce to your tutor that you want to work in a particular area but have done nothing personally to initiate enquiries. Moreover, if an employer receives scores of applications per day, as is certainly the case in, for example, the media industries, anything less than an impression of total dedication and self-motivation will be insufficient. If you think of it from the employers' perspective, enthusiasm, flexibility and initiative are excellent attributes in a student as with these three qualities in place the student is in a strong position to learn most other skills. Once you leave university, you will not have a tutor to help you apply for permanent work. You will rely on your own personal resources. With this in mind, it would be prudent to make the most of your tutor now in terms of the advice and guidelines (s)he is able to give you, so that by the time you leave university you are self-sufficient, you have thought through the issues that accompany looking for work and you have your own techniques and strategies to draw on. This in turn will give you more confidence in your own abilities and also greater overall independence and control over your future.

Putting oneself forward and drawing attention to a list of positive qualities may seem alien within some cultures, and indeed may not sit comfortably alongside British reticence and sang froid. However, students *need* to be able to highlight their skills, and more importantly, to articulate them to potential employers. If you are able to sell *yourself*, it is likely that you will be able to apply the same skills to a product, in that you will be able to research it, determine the selling features and articulate this persuasively to a third party. By presenting yourself in a good light, you are giving your potential employer a glimpse of some of the skills you can immediately bring to the workplace, so do not hide your talents and skills. However, remember to emphasise what you can do for them, rather than simply what you are good at, as this is what employers want to know most of all.

It is important to achieve a good balance between being ambitious in terms of what you want and being realistic. Do not be deterred by others if what you seek seems difficult to realise or indeed unattainable, but bear in mind that nothing short of 100 per cent effort will work in some circumstances. Going back to the example of media placements, whilst it is certainly true that most companies are oversubscribed and the majority of students will face disappointment at some point in the process, others will nevertheless achieve their goals. It is important to combine a positive approach with an acceptance that finding a placement is not necessarily going to be easy. Nearly all students will face rejection at some stage and it is important not to dwell on the negative side of this. Rejection should not be interpreted as a sign of personal failure. It is important to bear in mind that a more likely cause is the sheer number of applications. Rather than being downhearted at rejection, you could try to use the situation to your future advantage. If possible, ask for feedback on your application and be prepared to receive constructive criticism. If the problem is simply that you, like thousands of others, are aiming for organisations such as the national newspapers or television broadcasters, ask yourself what it is that you are hoping to learn, and see if there are some smaller organisations that can offer you similar experience, for example local newspapers, small independent producers or cable companies. A relevant work placement at this stage might be a stepping-stone to working in your first choice of organisation later, yet it may not be realistic in the first instance to aim for certain large organisations that are inundated with requests despite rarely or never offering placements. Alternatively, if you do decide to try a long-shot, give yourself a time limit after which you will abandon this particular quest and scale down your horizons, or you will simply waste time with no real likelihood of securing a placement. Whilst it is important to be optimistic and determined, it is also essential to be pragmatic and realistic.

▶ Constructing your curriculum vitae

In general terms, each application for a work placement will consist of a CV and a letter of application. You will probably be able to send the same CV to most organisations, although some minor adjustments may be required to emphasise and highlight relevant points. However, the letter of application should be tailored specifically to each organisation.

Points to include

Your generic CV should always include the following points: name; contact details including postal address, telephone number, mobile number and email address; date of birth; educational history and qualifications; employment history and qualifications (including key areas of responsibility if appropriate); interests and other relevant information. It may include a competence statement in which you outline your skills and attributes, and the names and contact details of two referees from whom you have sought permission to include, one of whom should be from your university. There are varying opinions as to whether to include a section on 'interests'. It can help to give a broader picture of the applicant, and can be used as a conversation opener in an interview situation, so it is wise to be truthful and only mention interests that you are genuinely able to talk about with enthusiasm and knowledge.

It is important not to clutter your CV with too much information. For example, it is normally sufficient to state the number of GCSEs you have gained without necessarily listing them. However, obviously if you have a GCSE in a subject relevant to your potential placement, and you do not have that subject at A level, then you might wish to draw attention to it. It is best to avoid unnecessary information, such as the words 'Curriculum Vitae' at the top of the page, and 'references will be supplied on request'.

There is a current vogue to print one's photograph on the CV, but this may detract from the professional tone. If a potential employer does require a photograph, s(he) is likely to request it.

Presentation and length

Opinions vary as to the ideal length of a CV. Some people prefer a CV that fits neatly into one page of A4, whereas others appreciate the additional information contained when it extends onto the second page. However, more than two pages is generally considered to be excessive, and runs the risk of not being read thoroughly.

It is important that the CV is pleasant to look at, with clear demarcation between various sections and a consistent style of headings and subheadings. In order to conserve space and to achieve an attractive look for the CV, it may be appropriate to organise some sections in the form of a table, such as employment history. Dates throughout should be in chronological order, beginning with the most recent. You may prefer to present information in brief bullet points and to expand on the relevant points in the accompanying letter.

Your CV should be word processed on good quality paper. Choose the font carefully; it should be easy to read, not too small, and ideally, match the font you select for the accompanying letter. You can vary the size to give emphasis to sub-headings if you wish. Don't cram everything in; be selective and allow the information sufficient surrounding space.

▶ Writing a covering letter

As I have noted, each covering letter should be individually composed for the organisation concerned. The rationale for this is that each company will regard itself as unlike others, and since a key feature of your application is to draw attention to what you in particular have to offer that company specifically, your letter must be customised.

The key purpose of the letter of application is to convey to your employer what you have to offer and why you wish to work for their organisation. Although altruism may play a part in your employer's willingness to accept a student into the workplace, (s)he is likely to be motivated primarily by what talents you can bring to the company and how you are able to contribute. It is very important to be enthusiastic and to have done your research about the company. Highlight any relevant experience you have, either in relation to your university course, past employment or education history, or interests. Make suggestions as to what you could contribute, but emphasise that you are prepared to be flexible and consider other options. Focus especially on your transferable skills as they mean that you are immediately useful in the workplace. In addition, list your personal attributes that you feel would be of benefit to the employer, particularly if your CV does not include a personal statement. Enquire if there are any discrete jobs that you could undertake, perhaps to clear a backlog. Although it is wise to be as flexible as possible, if you do have constraints in terms of when you need to undertake or complete the placement, it would be sensible to mention them in your letter. You might also mention what you hope to gain from the placement, together with any requirements from the university that involve the employer. End the letter by stating that you will telephone in a few days when they will have had time to consider your application. If you do not do this, you may find that your letter remains indefinitely in an in-tray and no action is taken on it.

Grammar and spelling are of the utmost importance in both the CV and the covering letter as care in these departments indicates that you are a thorough person with high standards. There is no excuse for poor spelling in today's era of computer spellcheckers! Also, remember to use the appropriate wording in your letter, that is, 'yours sincerely' if you have named the recipient, and 'yours faithfully' if you are writing to an unnamed person. And remember that it is always better to write to a specific person. Keep copies of all covering letters as, although they are individualised, you will be able to use the core paragraphs again with minor amendments.

▶ Filling in an application form

Some work placement schemes require the candidate to complete an application form. The layout is often partially tabulated which may make a typed response difficult. If you are called upon to fill in such a form it is essential to have a 'trial run' before undertaking a top copy, as otherwise you may find that your answers are too short, or worse, too long for the relevant boxes; you may make mistakes and the form may become messy. The best way of dealing with this situation is to photocopy the form and use the copy as a practice sheet. Once again, try to organise your answers into sections, perhaps using headings and bullet points. Sometimes applicants are directed to 'continue on a separate sheet if necessary'. However, if this offer is not made, it is best to tailor your answers to the space provided, unless you have vital information to divulge. Use a good quality pen, write in the same colour throughout and ensure that your writing is clearly legible. If you are asked not to include a CV with the form, do not include one!

▶ Telephone enquiries

If, rather than applying for an advertised work placement opportunity, you are 'cold calling' an organisation, it may be wise to make the initial contact by telephone, if only to determine whether or not the company concerned would consider offering work experience to a student. Write down the key points you wish to get across in the course of the telephone conversation and keep the list in view. You need to give your name, a contact number, and enough information about yourself to attract the attention of the listener. You need to communicate that you are a student looking for a work placement, plus a sentence about what you have to offer and a sentence pertaining to why you have selected this particular organisation. Keep the conversation concise and to the point. If you are not rebuffed, offer to post or to bring in your CV. You are likely to have to sell yourself well if you are to stand any chance of success, so choose a good time to make the call. Make sure that you are not likely to be interrupted, that you have your wits (and your list) about you, and try to speak confidently and clearly. Be prepared to leave a short message on a voicemail if it is required.

▶ Following up your application

Make sure that you can be contacted easily by the organisations to which you have applied. If you are going to be away, you should point this out in your covering letter. Make a point of checking your mobile telephone messages and emails once a day, and if possible ensure that your landline telephone is connected to an answerphone. There is nothing more likely to irritate a keen potential employer than being unable to make contact with you!

However, if you do not receive a response to your application it would be prudent to follow it up yourself and telephone the person concerned to enquire if they would be prepared to discuss it further or arrange a meeting. If they haven't got round to reading your application by this point, your call may prompt them to do so. If you glean this impression, you might offer to telephone again in a week. If you are able to create some sort of relationship with the person on the other end of the telephone, they are more likely to agree to a meeting or help you with alternative suggestions. It is essential that you note all developments in your placement notebook or computer file, particularly if you are leaving voicemail messages. Whilst it is important to get an answer, it is also wise not to pester the person concerned in such a way as to make them more reluctant to take your application further. If you note down each call, you will be able to judge this for yourself.

If after several weeks you have heard nothing, write again to the person concerned stating that you are still interested in a placement. However, if this second letter does not elicit a response, move on and target another organisation on your list. The first organisation may still reply with an offer, but you cannot be expected to wait indefinitely, and if in the meantime you have accepted another placement you have not behaved unprofessionally. Indeed, you should note the details of anything you are offered, but choose not to accept, because post graduation you may well wish to target the same people for more work. For this reason it would be prudent to write a letter saying that on this occasion you have accepted another placement, but reiterating your interest in the company and any suitable permanent vacancies that may arise there after your graduation.

If when you telephone you are turned down, take the opportunity to ask for suggestions as to where else to apply and ask if you might say who made the recommendation. Industry insiders are very well placed to know of potential vacancies elsewhere.

▶ Summary

This chapter has shown that organisational skills are vital in tracking applications for work placements, and that keeping a record of all correspondence and developments is essential. Finding a placement can be a lengthy process, punctuated by problems, so it is important to maintain a good attitude and not to be embarrassed about pointing out what you have to offer to potential employers. Having targeted an organisation, you should do some background research prior to filling in an application form or composing a CV and a covering letter, taking into account the guidelines indicated in this chapter.

Perspectives and Feedback

Avoid the same vague motivation that 95% of the applicants write, such as 'a placement in xxx would be the best way to put into practice what I have learned during the past years and would be a perfect match for both my academic background and personal interests'. This does not say anything about you and is not specific enough to draw the attention of those recruiting.

Jose, *employer – government*

In my experience students tend to highlight their part-time employment which is not always related to their degree course and placement. If they have had work experience in the [relevant] field we suggest that this should be on the first page of the CV. When students first give me their CVs they often list all their GCSE subjects and grades without giving sufficient details of their present degree course. Students to not always see the relevance of some of their own extra curricular activities. One particular student had been part of UK junior athletics for ten years before deciding to choose a university degree over a possibility of the British Olympic team trials. By not mentioning this on her CV, the dedication, commitment and hard work that she had shown throughout her formative years was not being highlighted as part of her personality.

Kay, *tutor*

Because we are a creative industry we are often pleasantly surprised with really innovative CV's. We have received everything from a CV attached to a brick, to chocolates, to a bottle of Flash in a saucepan with the note, 'I am not just a flash in the pan!' Those that make the effort to get creative are often more likely to get noticed. Your CV is 'you on paper' and the first contact you have with the prospective employer, so it is crucial that it is the best possible representation of you.

Celia, *employer – TV production*

I wouldn't have had a clue about how to write a CV and they gave us a sheet on it. I tried to highlight all the good points and not put anything negative. I tried to make myself look better.

Jessica, *student*

When you apply, make it clear what the course expects of the placement, and what you can offer. Don't forget about your previous experience as this may give you the advantage over other students applying from similar courses. Target organisations carefully and explain your reasons clearly and succinctly in your initial contact. Mass mailings may cast your net wider but will not necessarily help you find a placement. A focused approach is more likely to result in an offer of a placement that is right for you.

Caroline, *employer – human resources*

Occasionally you get a CV that stands out from the rest. It doesn't have to be gimmicky but it's a design job they are trying to get and yet some design their CV very badly. If they present themselves well they will really stand out.

Amanda, *employer – magazine*

Do sort out the CV, making sure you have a section on key skills. Have good – not standard – reasons why you've approached that particular organisation. In the nicest possible way try to remind the organisation you're trying to get into that they had to start somewhere too!

Annabel, *employer – PR*

It is important that the CV is individualised. If a company receives a batch of CVs that are practically identical then they will probably not be invited for an interview. If two friends prepare their CVs together and apply for the same placement the company will notice that they are similar. There is plenty of advice that can be found and Internet sites that will help you put a CV together, but an original CV will secure an interview. Students tend to view the CV as a report of their life, but should view it as an advert for themselves that highlights the points relevant to the particular position being sought.

Kay, *tutor*

4 Interview Success

This chapter will focus on:

- ▶ interview preparation
- ▶ interview protocol
- ▶ analysing your performance
- ▶ checking essential details before starting your placement

▶ Preparing for the interview

It is essential to be well-prepared both mentally and in a practical sense prior to attending an interview. Remember that an interview is basically an opportunity to sell a product – you! The packaging, that is, your appearance, is therefore very important, so give it due consideration. Your potential employer will form an impression of you from the way you look even before you say anything, and if you look smart and pleasant, it not only indicates that you are someone who possesses good presentation skills; it also shows that you want the job sufficiently to take the trouble necessary to secure it. Practical preparations for an interview include working out how you intend to travel to the interview and ensuring that you are clear about how long the journey is likely to take, making any wardrobe decisions, checking that all clothing is clean and ironed and gathering any literature that you may wish to take with you, such as relevant university projects.

In terms of mental preparation, you will already have a short file on the organisation, so it is advisable to reread it at this point, together with your original application, in order to refresh your memory. Pay particular attention to what the employer requires, remembering that this will be detailed in both the advertisement and the subsequent job and person specification. If you are being interviewed as a result of your own enquiries, and there is no paperwork, thinking about what the employer probably wants is still a good starting point. Begin by making a list of everything that you would like to convey to the employer in the course of the interview. This might include your previous experience, skills and personal qualities. It is quite possible that you might be asked at the end of the interview if there is anything you would like to raise that has not been covered, and this would give you a chance to mention any points on this list that have not been discussed.

Probably the best preparation is to think how you might answer some of the general questions that are likely to arise. In terms of the 'example' questions, it is wise to have more than one answer in case the question is asked in a different way more than once during the interview. Your answers should be concise yet not too short, and it may be beneficial to introduce an example to prove your point, particularly if you are asked if you possess a particular personal attribute, as by giving an example you are offering 'proof' of your ability. However, do not be tempted to try to mould your performance to fit what you think the employer wants, as this may simply generate the impression that you are trying too hard, especially if you are asked questions designed to provoke disagreement. It is important to be honest and to answer questions as accurately as you can, as this way your personality is more likely to shine through. Answer the questions that are asked, and not the questions that you would like to hear. Answer promptly if you are sure what you want to say, but do not be afraid to deliberate over deeper questions.

University careers advisors are very well placed to give general guidance on interview technique and to tackle specific areas of concern. Moreover, some students find it helpful to stage 'mock' interviews amongst themselves or with their tutor, or to talk to previous work placement students about their experiences of being interviewed. The best way of ensuring success is to prepare well.

Typical questions

As you enter the room, there will probably be some pleasantries that may touch upon your journey, your university and so on. These are designed to put you at your ease as the interview starts and they generally require very brief answers. However, be prepared to deal with some throwaway comments relating to the newspaper headlines or significant events of the previous day. For this reason it is always a good idea to glance at a newspaper on the way to the interview.

Other typical areas may include the following:

Q: Why did you apply to us?

A: Needs to cover reasons for interest in this industry in general and this organisation in particular, plus any relevant experience or skills. You will be able to use your background research findings in answering this question.

Q: What can you offer?

A: You should not only mention relevant work experience, but also course-related experience and transferable skills. Focus on your employability and usefulness.

Q: Do you have any previous experience?

A: If not, try to indicate skills that will now be useful although you may have gained them from completely different situations, such as dealing with members of the general public, telephone skills or managing a budget.

Q: What are your particular strengths and weaknesses?

A: Strengths as above. Include feedback from tutors and colleagues in your answer. Weaknesses – try to think of something that is not directly relevant to the job in question. Don't be tempted to claim that you don't have any weaknesses!

Q: Can you cope with tricky situations? Give an example.

A: Try to illustrate this with an example that shows a skill that is required in the work placement such as the ability to negotiate.

Q: What is the worst mistake you have made in your life?/Describe a highlight of your life?

A: Mistake – choose a mistake that will not deter the panel from employing you and make a point of stating what you learnt from the experience. Highlight – try to choose a highlight that shows personal development, and preferably something of use to this company. If you are simply choosing a 'happy moment', such as a family gathering, state what the event made you realise, for example, how fortunate you are to have a supportive family and what this means to you in terms of your outlook on life.

Q: How does the work relate to your university course?

A: If possible, give an example of how the practical nature of the work placement combines well with a theoretical aspect of your course to give a valuable overall picture, rather than attempting a lengthy evaluation that could become long-winded.

Q: What do you think you will be doing in ten years' time?

A: It is perfectly acceptable to answer this by saying that you are not sure, but you ought in that case to offer a few alternatives, for example, 'If I find that I do in fact want to pursue a career in clinical medicine, then I would hope that in ten years I shall be working as an ...' You might refer to the interim period and your immediate plans and state that the future is dependent on the outcome. Or, if you believe you know what you want already, do not be afraid to predict a rosy future for yourself within the appropriate industry.

In the course of your preparation, you may find it helpful to jot down some outline responses to the above questions. Once you are in the interview, the answers are likely to flow. You should also give some thought as to what questions you would like to ask, as there is likely to be an opportunity for this during the interview.

Questions for the employer

An interview is not a one-way situation. It gives you the opportunity to gain a better impression of the employer, just as it gives him or her the chance to find out more about you. Prior to attending the interview, you should consider what it is you want from an employer, and then use the situation to check any details you may still need in order to satisfy yourself that you are on the correct track to meet your own objectives. Do not ask for information that is readily available on their website, as you may be expected to know this already. However, you may wish to take this opportunity to clarify any points about the content of the work, or practical details such as timings and location, or what is required from the placement by your university, as misunderstandings at this stage are far easier to clear up than after the placement has commenced. Moreover, remember that whilst minor administrative matters can be dealt with once you have confirmation that the placement has been secured, if you have serious concerns, for example with regard to health and safety policies, you should raise them now. You may also wish to enquire about permanent work and training opportunities within the company. It not only gives a good impression that you are taking your placement seriously as a stepping-stone to your future career, but it also signals early on to the employer that you may wish to join permanently and that may prompt him or her to place you in a specific department, or to introduce you to relevant members of staff in the course of your placement so that they are able to form some sort of impression of you and your work whilst you are on the premises.

▶ Interview protocol

Ensure that you leave home for the interview in good time. It is essential to be punctual and arriving a few minutes early will mean that you have time to focus and calm down. If you are unsure of the journey, it is better to arrive early and go to have a coffee somewhere nearby rather than to have to rush and risk being late. You may wish to check your appearance prior to being shown to the interview room. Once there, be prepared to shake hands and do not take a seat until one is offered to you. Wait for the interviewer or panel to make the first move and try not to fidget or panic. It is wise to have extra CVs with you in case you are seen by a panel of people who otherwise need to share the one you sent in originally.

It is important to be honest and truthful as you answer the questions and if you do not understand a question there is no shame in asking for further clarification. Take your time if you need to deliberate before answering. Keep your answers to the point and do not be tempted to be too long-winded. Pick the salient points when answering and stop when you feel you have covered the question. Most interview candidates suffer a degree of nerves, no matter how experienced they are. The best counter measure to nerves is good preparation. If you are well-prepared, you are less likely to be floored by any questions and more likely to be able to turn the conversation to your own advantage. Nerves can also cause the candidate to try too hard! Try to remain focused on the question in hand and try to answer calmly and honestly.

It can be daunting to be faced with a panel, but the best approach is to focus on the person speaking to you. Address your answers to the person who asked the question. Do not worry if you cannot remember everyone's names and job positions. There will be further opportunities to ask to be reminded of these details if the placement goes ahead.

At the end of the interview it is courteous to thank the panel before you leave the room. If you are accepted for a placement, it is likely that you will receive notification of this in writing. If you receive a verbal acceptance, it is sensible to write back to the organisation thanking them for their offer and asking for clarification on any matters as yet unclear. It is very important that you receive some sort of a written contract outlining what the employer is expecting from you. You may well wish to write back politely pointing out your own expectations, including any university requirements. If this has been covered in the interview, you might flag this up by writing something along the lines of: 'To confirm what was discussed at our meeting last week …' before reiterating the details. There are far less likely to be problems if both parties are absolutely clear about what to expect. It is particularly important that you are aware of the nature of the work that you will be doing. If the employer has thought this through, he or she is likely to have lined up specific tasks for you, but if not, there is a danger that you will simply be given the tasks that nobody else wants to do. If this is discussed and confirmed in writing before you start, there is time for each side to offer alternative suggestions if the arrangements are not satisfactory.

If you are unsuccessful, it could be helpful to find out why, so it is a good idea to write to the interviewer, thank him for his/her time, and ask if (s)he is able to give you any advice or feedback that might help you in terms of future applications.

▶ Telephone interviews

Increasingly, telephone interviewing is becoming more important as a recruitment technique, and indeed, the Chartered Institute of Personnel and Development has noted a 10.9 per cent increase in the past year.[6] The main advantage to this form of interviewing is that it minimises discrimination in the absence of visual prompts as to identity, age and so on. Telephone interviews are also less disruptive and time-consuming. However, there are drawbacks, the most obvious being that the candidate is less able to get a feel for the organisation and is unable to test out some useful practicalities that may influence his or her view of the overall package, for example, the journey time and details. Moreover, some candidates will be less comfortable that others with the telephone medium.

In so far as work placement vacancies are concerned, employers may well decide to interview by telephone, particularly if it is logistically easier for them to do so, if the actual job relies heavily on a good telephone technique, or if the requirements can be determined from a person's CV beyond which the specification is very general. A key mistake made by telephone candidates is to rush their responses because they are not comfortable with silences on the line, whereas in person they might rely upon body language to indicate that they are deliberating on the question. If you are involved in a telephone interview, do not be afraid to take your time before delivering your answers. If you find the silences oppressive, make a comment that you would like a little time to consider your response, as this way you are signalling that you are focused on the question. You may also take notes if this helps you to formulate your responses. If you are telephoned at an inconvenient time when you are unable to give the call your undivided attention, ask for it to be rescheduled. If you are offered a work placement on the basis of a telephone interview, you should ask to visit the organisation at a later date as this will enable you to see the full picture and will safeguard against misunderstandings and misguided expectations.

▶ Analysing your performance

When you get home, find some time to write down your impressions of your performance in a reflective diary. You may soon find that you are in a position to assess your performance and criticise it constructively. Ask

---

[6] See Kate Hilpern, 'Clean break with tradition', *The Guardian Office Hours*, 13 October 2003, pp. 2–3.

yourself whether or not you were asked the questions you expected and how well you coped with them. Did you manage to include all the relevant information and were your answers of about the right length? Did you include all the points about yourself and your experience that you wanted to or did you leave out some important areas? Did any area of questioning go particularly well or particularly badly? How well did you cope with any feelings of nervousness? Overall, do you feel that you did justice to your skills, experience and personal attributes?

If you have attended more than one interview, you might find it useful to compare the comments you made of each experience in your reflective diary. Note particularly any recurring observations. If, for example, you have had problems in tackling a specific question more than once, it might help to write down a succinct answer to the question and practise it. If you stumbled over the examples you used to qualify your statements, this may indicate that you need to jot down a longer list so that you are more likely to remember enough information to support your arguments. If you can reflect upon your interview performance, identify the good and poor aspects of it, and think about how to improve your performance, your technique is likely to be better in the next interview. You may find it helpful to give yourself a personal mark for your performance and note it in your reflective diary if you feel that this will help you to remember each individual situation more clearly and compare two or more situations more easily. Hopefully you will notice an improvement as you gain interview experience.

▶ Dealing with negative experiences

It is very important to try not to become too dejected if you receive a number of rejections. Since finding a work placement is a very competitive process, it is actually quite likely that you will encounter rejection along the road to success. Try to accept this as part of the learning curve, and look upon writing applications and attending interviews as providing you with practice opportunities that will stand you in good stead in the future. If you remain focused and determined, success will eventually come your way. Later on, when you apply for various jobs in the course of your career, you will probably be grateful to have had a wide experience of being interviewed early on.

▶ Pre-placement checklist

By the time you are offered your placement, many of the details of it will be absolutely clear. You should know the times and dates, where you will be working, your duties, the dress code within the company and any remuneration including possible claims for meals and/or travelling expenses. In addition, you should ensure that the organisation has health and safety and equal opportunity policies, and that you have read them, that you are insured whilst in the workplace, and that you are aware of any tax or national insurance responsibilities you may have as a result of working. It is very important to be prepared, and if you can discuss your future placement with your tutor, peers or previous work placement students, you are far less likely to encounter serious difficulties.

Tax and national insurance

Work placement students are not normally liable for tax or national insurance simply because they do not usually earn enough income. In order to start paying tax you need to earn approximately £4,615 per annum, and national insurance contributions are required if weekly earnings are £89 or more.* If your earnings exceed these figures, you will need to pay tax and national insurance. In this instance, your organisation is likely to treat you as an employee and arrange this for you, although the responsibility to pay is yours. If you are paid, remember to collect a P45 form when you leave your placement as this contains evidence of any payments you have made. Further details may be found on: www.inlandrevenue.gov.uk

If you intend to work overseas, or if you are an overseas student working in the UK, there are several factors which influence whether or not you are eligible to pay tax and national insurance and the amount you may need to pay. Further details are available from the Centre for Non-Residents Helpline on 0845 070 0040. If you are telephoning from outside the UK, you need to dial the international code followed by 151 210 2222.

Insurance

You need to check that you are insured whilst at work. Your organisation should have employer's liability insurance and public liability insurance. Check that you are covered by these policies. If you are not insured, it is very inadvisable to work.

Health and safety

All organisations are required by law to have a health and safety policy and on arrival for work you should be advised of fire and emergency procedures. Make sure that you are aware of the location of fire exits, fire extinguishers and the assembly point in the event of a fire drill. In addition,

---

* Figures are for 2003–4.

ensure that you are introduced to the fire warden and first aid warden for the area in which you will be working. Check if any areas of the organisation pose particular dangers and should not be entered and ask if you need any protective equipment or clothing, for example, a hard hat. If you have any doubts at all about any aspects of your duties or working environment, you should speak to your health and safety representative.

Equal opportunities

Equal opportunities legislation is in place to ensure that people are protected from discrimination on the grounds of sex, race or disability. However, the emphasis on this varies from company to company and you may wish to seek further clarification from the Personnel Officer prior to accepting a work placement.

For home students going overseas

Generally, students undertaking work placements in other EU countries do not require permits, whereas those working outside the EU need specific documentation. However, to be on the safe side, it is best to check with the embassy of your chosen country regarding what you will require. Students working abroad should ensure that they have adequate insurance cover that will suffice in the worst case scenario. In addition to covering possessions, tickets, money and so on, it should include full accident and medical cover that would provide for an air-ambulance home if required, and cover any transportation costs in the event of death. Ideally it would also include third party liability cover.

Overseas students working in the UK

Although it is no longer a requirement for students from non-EU countries to be in possession of a work permit in order to undertake a work placement, there are still some restrictions in place and it is wise to check the Home Office guidelines before finalising arrangements. The following website gives further information about which students from overseas do and which do not need permission to work: www.workingintheuk.gov.uk

▶ Making other arrangements

Clearly, undertaking your work placement will be time-consuming. If you are attending your placement one day each week, that effectively means that you will have to fit all your other work and personal arrangements into one day less, and if your placement is full-time you will have little available time for anything else. It is therefore a good idea, prior to starting your work placement, to consider your circumstances and to reschedule your arrangements wherever necessary. In the case of university commitments, tutors of other modules are likely to be sympathetic if you advise them in advance of specific busy times. They may agree to give you reading lists early, for example, so that you can make a start prior to the relevant course commencing. It is always best to anticipate potential problems that may arise from a clash of dates, such as being asked to hand in a piece of written work in the middle of a full-time placement, as with forward planning and negotiation, difficult situations can normally be avoided.

Similarly, you may wish to review your social commitments during your work placement period, not simply because the work may prove physically and intellectually tiring, but also because it is a good idea to be flexible about the time you need to leave work. It is sensible to allow yourself a sufficient gap after your agreed working hours to finish off an urgent task or to join other members of staff for a social occasion that may arise at the last minute.

▶ Summary

This chapter has focused on the interview situation and the preparations necessary before starting a placement. Prior to attending an interview, bear in mind the questions likely to be asked and jot down short outline answers. Your interview performance is likely to improve with practice, particularly if you keep a reflective diary of your experiences and look back over the entries from time to time. If you are offered a placement make sure that you are clear about all the arrangements and use the checklist to ensure that you have covered the most important areas.

Perspectives and Feedback

One of the students was completely thrown by the formality of the initial interview she had to attend to obtain the placement, so a thorough briefing by the workplace co-ordinator is necessary.

Clare, *tutor*

It can be very disappointing when students arrive for an interview and haven't researched the company at all. For example when asked which programmes of ours they enjoy watching the most, they can't name one! On the whole though, as the industry is a fairly easy one to follow (one only has to watch television to be up to speed) they are usually extremely well prepared.

Celia, *employer – TV production*

I didn't have any practice interviews. I've always enjoyed speaking to people or having interviews so I just went along. I made sure that I knew exactly what I had written on the application form. I also made a double check just to read the paper on the morning, just to have some extra examples to talk about. Otherwise I didn't do much preparation.

Thomas, *student*

One student forgot to bring their CV with them to the interview which put them at an immediate disadvantage. I just thought that was completely ridiculous! It showed that they didn't have a clue. I said: 'This is an interview. Didn't you think to bring your CV?' They just mumbled and apologised.

Amanda, *employer – magazine*

Offices often are visited by clients, staff therefore need to look presentable (i.e. clean clothes). Alternatively, staff need to leave the building to meet suppliers and/or clients so should be presentable enough to be representative of their company. So when senior managers meet a prospective employee they want to see in front of them a potential colleague for whom they do not need to apologise or feel embarrassed. If you don't have a clean, ironed pair of trousers, shirt, skirt or whatever, borrow one. Nobody was ever rejected for having clothes that were not a perfect fit. Dirty, ripped, worn out or 'cheap fashion', however contemporary, don't impress.

Michael, *employer – conferences and exhibitions*

My interview was quite informal and comfortable. I felt confident in that I had taken initial ideas with me. These showed my initiative and I think they were impressed by that.

Judi, *student*

They [interview candidates] are a bit monosyllabic. They tend to give a lot of yes/no answers and are not pro-active in their questioning. They sit there, mute, and do not ask questions in return to yours. They tend not to show enthusiasm. It really is about doing your homework before you arrive so that you can show a bit of nous. It is almost always immediately obvious who will and who will not be right for the job.

Marie, *employer – advertising*

My interview was organised at short notice, as was the placement. For this reason I didn't have a huge amount of time to prepare. I made sure my clothes were smart but also appropriate for being outdoors. I was asked what aspects of the [open air] museum I was interested in, and was given a tour of the site so I would know my way around, which I found useful. Any questions I had were answered and I was shown where to sign in every morning.

Emily, *student*

Common civility such as using old fashioned phrases such as 'please' and 'thank you', turning up on time and having done a bit of recent relevant research into the company who are interviewing you will go down well.

Michael, *employer – conferences and exhibitions*

I would always wear a suit no matter what it was I was going for, because you don't know what they are expecting, and if you turn up and they are dressed down, then that's fine – you can dress down when you get the job. But you need to look professional and it does make a difference I think. I wouldn't take the risk of dressing down, just in case.

Amelia, *student*

5 Getting the Most Out of Your Placement

This chapter will focus on how you can get the most out of your placement by:

- ► keeping track of your objectives
- ► maintaining a good attitude
- ► learning from individuals and group situations
- ► honing your current skills and developing new ones
- ► welcoming new experiences
- ► making contacts for the future
- ► reflecting on your experiences

In order to get the best out of your placement, it is essential that both you and your employer are clear as to what you will be doing, the hours you will be working, the person to whom you will be responsible, and any relevant terms and conditions relating to your placement period. Before you commence work, these details should have been committed to paper so that you each have a record of what has been discussed. On receipt of this information you should reflect on your expectations, and if possible discuss them with your placement tutor. If you are well-prepared for what you will encounter, you are likely to be more confident and comfortable in the workplace. Prior to starting your placement, it is wise to remind yourself of your objectives and think through the process of achieving them. It is likely that you will hope to learn new skills and practise and improve those you already have; learn about workplace culture and protocol; find out more about yourself and what you may or not want in terms of your future career and make contacts that may help you in the future.

The key to achieving these objectives lies primarily in your attitude to your work placement and your ability for self-reflection and self-evaluation. It is important to be flexible as this will not only make you more useful from the point of view of work colleagues, but will also increase the potential for encountering new situations and experiences. Enthusiasm and hard work are likely to be rewarded by respect and increased responsibility, and if you are willing to learn the procedures preferred by your organisation you will quickly make a valuable contribution. Think of it from your employer's point of view – if a worker is keen and takes pride in the work (s)he does, the product is likely to have a better finish, and if the worker is responsive to guidance and suggestions then he or she is very likely to be able to adopt the 'house style' of working that will assist the integration of both the person concerned and the output. Similarly, if all employees maintain a pleasant, professional outlook it will ensure that the office runs smoothly and that a good atmosphere prevails. Hopefully, you will quickly be able to draw on your skills and personality to make a positive contribution to work related issues.

▶ Learning from your work placement

The potential for learning exists in many aspects of the working environment and it may be useful to consider the various elements and how well they apply to your particular situation. These include learning by observation; learning through practice; facing new experiences; learning through feedback and self-reflection; and building up contacts and networks.

Learning from individuals/shadowing

Do not underestimate the value of learning from shadowing a colleague. As your mentor goes about her daily duties, you will be able to build up a picture of how this section of the organisation works. Not only will you gain insight into the role played by various departments and individuals, but you will also see how one specific job breaks down into various components, whilst observing the time spent on each aspect of the job and the skills required. In addition you will be able to judge how well or badly the individual concerned tackles the various aspects of the job and you are likely to be able to learn new techniques for coping in similar situations. It does not matter whether you are presented with a skilful mentor who rarely makes mistakes or with someone whose performance leaves a great deal to be desired, so long as you continually observe what is happening and analyse in your own mind what works well and what does not, you will learn from the experience. You will be able to learn a great deal from watching the actions of those around you and you may pick up useful tips, such as how to deal with difficult clients on the telephone, how to diffuse a tricky situation, how to conduct research in a particular area or other job specific skills.

Learning from group dynamics

You can learn a considerable amount from both observing group dynamics and also from assessing your own contribution. Most organisations have at their core a notion of teamwork being integral to progress, either in terms of making a product or in terms of sharing and building on ideas. Whilst observing a meeting or interaction in the office, ask yourself who is able to communicate their ideas and views well, and then try to analyse why this person is successful in this sense. You now have an opportunity to witness communication skills in action. Do participants in meetings communicate their views using background statistics and research, power of oration, bullying techniques or a combination of all of these? How do different people tackle the same problem and which tactics work best? Do people speak as individuals and then argue their case if they encounter objection or do they solicit the views of their colleagues during the course of the debate? Which types of comments are immediately shot down and which become the focus for further discussion? If you observe and learn, you will find it easier when the time comes to make your own contribution.

Workplace culture and protocol

Employers need staff who will fit well into the workplace and who will find it a stimulating yet comfortable environment in which they can utilise their skills and resources to best advantage. At first glance, the ability to integrate within an organisation seems fairly straightforward. However, it actually calls upon a high level of social and communication skills and it is an area in which experience of the workplace certainly helps. There may appear superficially to be a great deal of freedom in the workplace in that, for example, individuals decide what to wear to work, what time to arrive and depart, when to take their lunch break, when it is appropriate for conversations to change from work-based issues to personal ones and how best to tackle their daily tasks. However, these choices are rarely as open ended as they may at first appear. Although the 'rules' are not explicit, there is usually an unspoken, subtle agreement as to the correct protocol and the range of possibilities permitted within it, although this will vary from business to business. If you think this is not the case in your organisation, look at examples of behaviour that have met with disapproval and the invisible guidelines will become apparent. People who operate outside this area may become isolated and may find that they are irritating, upsetting or alienating their colleagues. It is very important to observe the office etiquette and make sure that your own actions and behaviour are appropriate. This should not be seen as restrictive, but as an acknowledgement of the prevailing office culture and a willingness to act with due consideration for colleagues. Since it takes time to work out what is and what is not acceptable, it is generally wise to observe quietly when you first arrive in the workplace, rather than trying to make an immediate impression. Note particularly whether it is best to make yourself scarce at lunchtime or whether you are expected to join in, and the general level of formality or informality within the office.

Relationships are important and friendship groups are likely to meet socially outside office hours. The social and personal conversations within the office are fundamental to establishing each person's individuality and to maintaining a rapport within the team and a supportive and pleasant atmosphere. It is very important that you are always able to maintain a professional relationship within the workplace and that you are able to reach an appropriate balance in terms of contributing to the sociable atmosphere of the office whilst getting your work done. It is also important that you are able to work with everybody with whom your job calls for you to collaborate. It is not wise to allow personal feelings to interfere in your professional dealings; you need to be able to work with and maintain a professional relationship with people you do not like as well as those who are or may become friends.

Office politics exist in every organisation and whilst it is good to be aware of what is going on, active involvement in terms of taking sides, gossiping or making inappropriate comments is likely to damage your own reputation as a professional and adversely affect your work. Moreover, the workplace operates on the basis of inequality of status and there is normally a clearly-defined hierarchy. Custom and practice in the office may dictate which members of staff mix with each other socially. This situation is a fact of life and you will need to learn how to deal with those in authority, your peers, and those who expect guidance from you. It is essential that you are able to maintain your professionalism, whatever is going on around you. The work placement situation is different to that of full-time employment in that the student is perceived as someone who is in a learning situation. This may excuse you from aspects of the normal protocol in the sense that you will be in a position to approach those much higher up the company for advice or information. You may therefore be seen as akin to a management trainee, although others may afford you no status at all on the basis that you do not have a 'real' job there. You may find it helpful to think through how others may perceive and treat you before you arrive, so that you are prepared.

Since it is important that you are not set apart from the prevailing office culture during your work placement, but are gradually accepted as part of it, it is important to try to assess the situation as soon as you can. You are likely to be introduced to many new people when you first start and you may find it helpful to jot down their names, to avoid the embarrassment of having to ask again if you forget. If you also make a note of their extension numbers and areas of responsibility, you will know who to ask if you have a query. It is likely that once you are established you will then be included in the more social side of work life, such as joining colleagues during the lunch break. However, bear in mind that this may take time.

Your experience of office culture whilst on work placement offers two key benefits. First, it means that you are aware of the subtle rules and conventions that underpin organisations in general and your specific company in particular, and that you are likely to have practised your own social and interpersonal skills in integrating within your own work environment. From a future employer's perspective, this makes you more employable. However, secondly it gives you the opportunity to consider your long-term requirements. What do you like and dislike about the atmosphere at your work placement? Are you comfortable with a formal or an informal situation? Do you enjoy working alone or as part of a team? Is interaction with your colleagues one of the most stimulating aspects of working or is it irrelevant to how you feel at the end of the day? The answers to these questions will help you with decisions when you face future career choices.

Encountering new experiences

Hopefully, your work placement will enable you to encounter many new experiences, especially if you are in an industry about which you know very little. Once you feel comfortable with your day to day work, do not be reluctant to ask to see other departments in order to get a comprehensive picture of the company. It may be that viewing the various processes involved in producing the finished result brings life and meaning to the small task that is your own contribution. If you are, for example, working in a record company, ask if you may observe a press conference, or a record being made. If you are marketing an industrial product, ask to see the factory so that you have an idea of the scale and complexity of the process. Similarly, a tour of your building may give you an essential overview. Do not be afraid to ask for something that will clearly contribute to your learning experience, but be prepared to do this in your own time if necessary. It will pay dividends later as it will give you a much deeper understanding of the workings of the company, and you are likely to be able to refer to this in subsequent career-related interviews.

Apart from the obvious examples of new experiences that you will encounter in the workplace, there are also personal dilemmas that are equally valuable to your learning, for example, how you deal with being given too much or too little work, how you face difficult situations, and so on. These call upon skills that you will need throughout your working life, and encountering these and similar situations during the relative safety of your work placement enables you to test yourself in a learning situation when mistakes and miscalculations are to be expected to a certain degree and you are still able to draw on support from your tutor and peers.

Practising skills
Many skills develop and improve as a result of practice, and a work placement presents an ideal opportunity to hone skills. This applies to both practical skills such as operating computer packages, conducting research and writing reports plus 'soft' skills such as interacting with colleagues in an appropriate way and working efficiently as part of team. Sometimes it is quite difficult to determine whether or not there has been an improvement. It may be useful to consider whether or not you are able to perform tasks more quickly or with fewer mistakes. Your own personal 'barometer' may help you in assessing the degree of comfort you have in a given situation. It may be that tasks which at first caused you concern, such as dealing with clients on the telephone, may now, due to practice, no longer be a cause of worry, or that you are now able to act on your own initiative with confidence, whereas before you may have had to seek guidance. Try to find some way of measuring your achievements as this will enable you to develop your skills more quickly and successfully.

The value of feedback
Feedback can be extremely valuable, but only if it is interpreted as constructive advice rather than simply as criticism. It is always difficult to ask for feedback since this makes you vulnerable to adverse comments about your performance and personality. However, try to rise above this and see objectively what problems your critic has with your work. If there is truth in the comment and you can see this for yourself, then it is very likely that you will be able to overcome the problem and improve your performance. Try not to take feedback too personally – you are learning and therefore cannot be expected to get everything right at this stage. However, since you are in the early stages of your career, you also have the flexibility to change and improve as you are unlikely to be set in your working ways. Do not dwell on what are your perceived failings but try to think of ways to alter the situation. If the answer is not immediately apparent, ask your critic for his or her opinions on this. If asking for feedback seems too personal, you might start a suggestion book, in which people might write pieces of advice. This objectifies the process of pointing out mistakes and as such de-personalises it.

Self-reflection as a lifelong learning resource
You are most likely to learn from your work placement if you spend time reflecting upon each aspect of it, and particularly if you then analyse your

response and reaction to the various situations you encounter and think through how your behaviour and performance could be improved. Self-reflection is in itself an acquired skill as criticising your own performance, particularly when you feel it may have been adversely affected by the actions of others, is not a natural reaction. It is important to try to be as objective as possible in assessing a specific situation, both in terms of evaluating what others have said and done and the underlying rationale for this, and in terms of your own response. Even if someone else initiated a problem, with hindsight it might be that you are able to discern how a different course of action on your part would have helped the situation. If you are able to achieve this, you will be able to use the lessons of each particular incident in tackling a similar situation in the future. Reflection is the vital link that connects theory and practice in that it is an intellectual exercise the result of which is to make sense of events. If you are able to master self-reflection and self-evaluation you will have the benefit of a lifelong learning resource at your fingertips throughout your career.

Over time, developing the skill of self-reflection can help you to understand more about yourself. It is important to get beneath superficial characteristics and discover what really motivates you, how your thought processes work in terms of analysing a situation and deciding what to do next and how this affects your behaviour and performance. It is useful to know how you appear to others, and why, as this may mean that minor modifications in the way you approach certain situations will improve the likelihood of a successful outcome. If you are aware of your strengths and weaknesses you will be able to seek training that can build on the former and improve the latter.

Although the key to achieving this level of self-awareness is honesty, you also need a strategy that will enable you to monitor and measure your progress. The best way to keep a track of your self-evaluative skills is to keep a diary or log in which to write about the events of the working day and your responses. It would be wise to do this whether or not it is a requirement of your university, as it is an excellent way of organising your self-reflection and evaluation. In Chapter 10, I shall outline how to initiate and maintain a learning log, and indicate what sort of information and analysis it should ideally contain. The main purpose of the log is to identify and highlight your own personal development in the workplace by charting the highs and lows, your immediate response, your views of the same incident after reflection, and most importantly, how you react when a similar situation arises again. Honing your self-evaluative skills should give you more confidence in yourself and your abilities, and should enable you to analyse and improve your performance within the workplace.

Support from your university

It is advisable to stay in touch with your work placement tutor and fellow students whilst on placement, and if you encounter any problems that you are not able to resolve yourself, to seek a solution through discussion, or possibly through role-play as this will point out all the different perspectives involved. Sometimes it is easier to envisage the best course of action when you are not too closely involved, but in any case, your tutor is likely to have experience of finding solutions to the most common problems. If you can arrange to meet your fellow students once in a while to discuss your feelings about your placements, this is likely to prove very useful. Not only will it confirm that some experiences and problems are common to many placements, but it will also offer the opportunity of discovering other people's solutions and coping strategies. Once you are in the workplace after graduation, you will need to rely on your own self-evaluative skills. However, whilst you are still at university, your tutor and peers will be able to give you useful feedback that is 'safe' in that it can remain confidential and is offered by those who know you but who are unconnected to your workplace. You may wish to discuss your key observations from your learning log with your tutor and peers as their feedback may in turn open your mind to new interpretations.

In some universities, the work placement module is designed to involve a visit by the tutor during the placement at which point meetings with both the student and the employer may take place on site. You can use this to your advantage. If you are having any specific problems, such as with the level of the work you are being given, your tutor will be able to raise this as a point of discussion at the meeting. Therefore, it is a good idea to reflect upon any areas of dissatisfaction in advance and to ensure that your tutor is aware of them. Try to present them in a positive way at the meeting, such as, for example, by stating that you would welcome further challenges. Try to include the positive points too, for example by mentioning work you have particularly enjoyed and by giving an indication of what you have learnt. Try not to regard this meeting as an ordeal but as an opportunity to use your negotiating skills to secure an arrangement that you may find of greater benefit. This is your opportunity to take your work placement in a different direction.

Networking and making contacts

It is wise to begin a 'contacts book' when starting your work placement, most particularly if, after leaving university, you hope to develop your career in the same industry or profession. Some people like to use a filofax for this, whilst others prefer an a–z book. Whilst it is useful to have both a hard copy and one on the computer, it is not wise to keep only a computerised record as you may need to refer to the entries when you are away from the office or when it is inconvenient to start up your computer. The same contacts book should serve for several years so it is better to reserve it for work details rather than including those of friends and family. You never know when you might wish to call up somebody you met or spoke to on your work placement so write down all contacts that may be of use later, particularly people with whom you had a good rapport. Do not restrict it to those within your placement organisation, but include those outside the company with whom you had dealings. When you are job hunting after graduation, your contacts and networks could prove invaluable.

The immediate future
In the immediate future some students may have to submit written assignments and projects in connection with their placement. Do not lose sight of this if it applies to you. Think about the assignments while you are on placement as it is a great deal easier to research aspects of the organisation from within. Also, if you are planning a presentation or a report, consider whether the use of graphics and illustrations will make your assessed work more interesting and if so, look for suitable leaflets, pictures, graphs and so on whilst you are there in person. You may also wish to ask key members of staff for short quotations that you can use in your work, or to take photographs of the office in action. It will be much more difficult to obtain this type of data after you have left.

Before you leave, make sure that you have contact numbers for colleagues with whom you have a good rapport and those who may be able to help you in the future. Ask one or two senior people if they would be prepared to give you a reference in the future when you are applying for permanent work, and after you have left remember to write and thank those within the organisation who helped you with your placement.

▶ **Summary**

This chapter has examined how students can get the most out of their placements, and has suggested that they may need to look beyond their immediate duties in order to maximise the experience. It has emphasised that learning about one particular business and a set of skills relating to a specific job is important, but that it only represents the tip of the iceberg. In addition, students should expect to learn from observing others in the workplace as this will enable them to develop an understanding of workplace culture and dynamics. Students may reasonably hope to encounter new experiences, practise skills they already have, develop new skills and make contacts for the future during their work placement. Key to achieving this is an appropriate attitude, an awareness of the need for flexibility, and a willingness to use self-evaluation and self-reflection in order to improve performance.

Feedback and Perspectives

When a placement goes well, it has such a super, motivating effect on the student. They begin to see how their academic studies are part of the preparation for their working life. They get a sense of working towards a goal. The contact with non-academics can teach them so much too. They usually take so much more notice of advice or criticism from employers than from tutors. A student who went to xxx got involved in quite hard physical work at which she would have turned her nose up normally, but there she was part of the team and would not let her team down. It was very good for her, as she had a rather inflated sense of her own importance before she went.

Jenny, *tutor*

To begin with I was unsure of what to do with my lunch break – I had an hour, and wasn't sure if I was expected to eat with the staff or not. For the first couple of days I took a book and sat on a bench in the woods (the site was on 45 acres). However, on the third day, my supervisors asked if I would join them at the café. It turned out that the whole team lunched there, and although I enjoyed my reading time, I'm sure that being with everyone else chatting over lunch helped me settle in. I found everyone very friendly and interested in what I had to say which really made me feel part of the group. I really enjoyed my time. This is mainly due to the fact that my supervisors gave me worthwhile things to do – not just jobs that no one else wanted.

Emily, *student*

Generally greater value was achieved if the student worked in a placement that was closely associated with their course work. We tended to offer more interesting work to marketing students, e.g., marketing research, competitor analysis and case studies. However if the student was crossing over to marketing and had little course work experience then they were more likely to receive mundane tasks like database building – of little value to them but still important to us. Placement managers are likely to give more responsibility to a student who has performed his/her tasks accurately, fast and to a high standard. More responsibility will undoubtedly mean more interesting tasks.

Alistair, *employer – marketing for new media*

We developed a detailed work programme. I made sure that I got on with everyone and helped out wherever I could. No airs and graces! And I just listened to/questioned what was going on around me. It was great just to get involved with a small organisation where you could see everything that was going on.

Mark, *student*

Students must be aware that whilst they may be focused on their quali- fications and career, they can also learn from the expertise and years of practical work experience of those in the workplace. A lack of respect for colleagues will not prove conducive to the placement. Students must also be able to see the bigger picture: Work placement projects may not necessarily be identified by the student as high profile and 'sexy' but may be absolutely essential to the routine maintenance of the organisa- tion, for example storage projects and audits.

Sally, *employer – museum*

I would agree that placements can be highly beneficial for those of us who don't know what we really want to do, but I also know of a lot of people who have had their hearts set on specific careers only to find that in reality, they hate the work! In my placement (although it was only short – 4 months), I made an effort every week to discuss my new ideas. I also regularly spoke to management for feedback on my work and progress. I think this helped – I built close relations with other members of the team and I think this helped us to be more honest. I did feel like part of the team and I think this was mainly due to my openness and willingness to learn. I would stress that placement students should remember that they are there to learn, and not go in to the job thinking that they know it all!

Arabella, *student*

Recognise that the world of work is not the same as university. Employer's expectations are high and this requires great levels of per- sonal commitment and enthusiasm. Just because you are the placement student does not mean that you can act in an unprofessional manner. Always make time to reflect on what is actually happening as the placement progresses. There is little point in reflecting at the end of the placement on what went well and what did not. Personal reflection in real time is the only way to maximise the learning opportunities. Finally, always remember that the placement is YOURS, not your placement employer's nor the university's. Take personal responsibility for what you get out of the placement, ensure that your goals are achieved and you will be advantaged in more ways than you can imagine.

Derek, *tutor*

My feeling after my work experience [on a newspaper] was that it was not very relevant to what I wanted to be, but it increased my confidence and self-esteem.

Charlotte, *student*

Make the most of the placement/project manager's skills and experience. Most will have signed up to the placement because they are committed to providing the best possible work experience for the individual and not because they want a 'basket carrier'. Once in an organisation, don't subvert a placement by approaching another department you may be more interested in – it will engender bad feelings between yourself and your host department. People in an organisation do talk and this type of behaviour will affect future placements.

Sarah, *employer – museum*

[The first day] I was so scared of doing something stupid that I sat in a corner and didn't say anything. However, during the second day I discovered that everyone was friendly and they weren't judging me on everything I did. On the third day I was in the sound department learning how they put the sound on [film].

Lauren, *student*

I gained a realistic insight to the magazine office environment. By spending time with other journalists I was able to make critical judgments on their working style, attitudes to work (very hardworking), and to observe their interactions among other staff. I was also lucky enough to get time to receive comments and advice from the associate editor who told me how to pitch my ideas and how to improve my writing style. The magazine was very busy and therefore [staff were] not so attentive to me, but I didn't expect them to be. It lowered my confidence at times but I saw this as a valuable exercise in overcoming some of my over-sensitive tendencies which I know are not compatible within a journalistic environment. I was sent to the premiere of *The Italian Job* on my own to report on the story, interview actors and write up the story for the following day. I experienced the pressure to deadlines as well as the excitement first hand. The mistakes I made, such as asking the wrong actor the wrong question, enhanced my learning experience. I was proud of myself for coping with it and smiling.

Judi, *student*

Advice to other students – research your placement in advance, so you can impress. Companies see a lot of placement students, so you have to stand out. If you show enthusiasm and are hard working (like you would be in a paid job) you will be rewarded. OVER DELIVER! That's what my Dad told me and it was the best advice I've been given. Don't feel bad when you're left with nothing to do, take this opportunity to explore your surroundings, read a book, make yourself a cup of tea! Make notes of what you do and who with, you never know when they may come in useful (e.g., writing essays/writing CVs, applications/interviews)

Kelly, *student*

6 Common Problems Facing Students

This chapter will:

- ▶ focus on the need to manage expectations
- ▶ identify common problems for students
- ▶ discuss how to prevent problems
- ▶ suggest remedial strategies

▶ Managing expectations

Many work placement problems arise when the student's expectations are not met. This may stem from a mismatch of aims and expectations between employer and student, or it may occur because the student may have an unrealistic picture of life on placement and is therefore very likely to be disappointed with the reality. Perhaps this is unsurprising when a work placement represents a new experience for most students, and it is one to which many look forward as being the first step on the career ladder. Reflecting on the proposed situation prior to the placement starting is invaluable, as if the student embarks upon the placement with realistic expectations, not only is he or she less likely to be disappointed, but also, with this outlook the student is more likely to be able to see and take advantage of the underlying benefits of the situation in addition to the more obvious learning opportunities. It is essential, therefore, that students take the time before starting the placement to think through their expectations, and if possible to discuss these with their tutor. Talking to previous work placement students about their experiences may also be very useful.

▶ Common problems

Generally, problems tend to arise in connection with the nature, level and quantity of the work, as a result of interpersonal concerns in the workplace, or due to practical issues. In this chapter, these areas will be addressed individually.

▶ Concerns about the work

Nature of the work
Sometimes problems begin to brew even before the placement starts, most particularly if for one reason or another the student is not convinced that (s)he has found an appropriate placement that matches career aspirations and personality. These nagging doubts can grow and may have a detrimental effect. This is more likely when the student has been very enthusiastic about a placement in a specific sector in which it has not been possible to secure a position, and has then opted for an alternative position. It may also occur if the student has no specific reason for accepting the placement because (s)he is unsure both of preferred future career direction and perhaps also which personal attributes and skills are likely to generate the greatest feelings of work satisfaction.

Some students find that the nature of the work is not what they expected and that because of this it is unfulfilling, or, even worse, that they are uncomfortable engaging in it. Sometimes career plans are rapidly revised in the course of a work placement simply because assumptions about the nature of the work involved have proved incorrect and disappointing.

Level of work
A common source of anxiety for students stems from being given work of an inappropriate level. This can be at either extreme of the scale. On the one hand students may find themselves facing assignments that they do not know how to tackle. Tasks may seem complex and require knowledge of 'house' style and processes. Moreover, if they call for interaction with other staff, this may pose a problem in that a new person might not necessarily know the most appropriate member of staff with whom to liaise. In either case the student will probably feel frustrated and perhaps intimidated. On the other hand, the workload may mainly comprise boring, repetitive tasks that do not utilise the student's skills, and when engaged in such duties for more than a short time this is likely to incite feelings of boredom, despondency and demoralisation. Having either too much work

or too little work may lead to feelings of isolation, particularly if other staff seem fully occupied with their own concerns.

Frequently, students expect to be given an interesting project on arrival at their placement. Whilst this can and does happen, it would be unrealistic to presume that this is always the case as, unless the student concerned already knows a great deal about the sector and organisation, he or she is unlikely to have the essential basic background knowledge that is necessary if one is to embark upon a complex assignment. Many students complain about being given menial tasks to do such as filing and answering the telephone. However, if you think of the placement as an apprenticeship, these tasks offer an introduction to the company whilst allowing you to settle in and get to know the other personnel together with how the department works. If you do the filing well and your employer knows that you can be trusted to be efficient and maintain a positive attitude, you are far more likely to be promoted to other tasks. Whilst work placement students should not expect to have to do menial tasks at all times, it is not unreasonable to be directed to undertake simple tasks during the settling in process and from time to time afterwards. Answering the telephone, another 'basic' task, is actually a good way of getting to know who everyone is and what they do. Moreover, whilst undertaking undemanding tasks, the student has more opportunity to observe and learn from others in the workplace and assimilate a clear picture of the situation. It comes as a surprise to some students that all jobs have their less exciting aspects, and that these have to be dealt with alongside the more challenging and rewarding tasks. It is unrealistic for students to assume that menial tasks will not form any part of their work, either during the placement or in the future, but it is important to negotiate an appropriate balance of tasks with the employer.

Quantity of work
Problems may also arise as a result of the quantity of work that the student is expected to undertake, and this too presents difficulties at either end of the scale. If you are given too much to do and too many demands are made on your time, the unfortunate result is that you will not be able to produce your best work. Indeed, if you are over-stretched, you are unlikely to have the time to do anything well, which in turn increases anxiety and reduces job satisfaction. For a work placement student, this situation is often compounded by lack of knowledge about the running of the organisation as this can mean that it is very difficult to prioritise tasks. You may also find that you feel pressurised to work overtime in order to finish work that you have been given, or to help colleagues if a crisis occurs. The converse situation is having little or nothing to do or having large gaps in between

tasks. Students in this situation are likely to feel demoralised as their skills are not being put to use and they are unable to make a valid contribution to the overall output. They may justifiably feel angry and frustrated. Also, it is embarrassing to be idle in a busy working environment when others seem fully occupied, and the effect is isolating.

Level of competence

It is important to remember that the work placement is a learning experience and students are not expected to be able to cope with everything from the outset. Some students forget this and become unhappy because they frequently have to ask for help or because they do not know how to tackle the tasks set for them, and this makes them feel stupid. Some students find it so overwhelming that they do not wish to continue. There is a great deal to learn when you enter a new environment, especially at the beginning, and most people are not able to take in everything at once. You may find it helpful to jot down the names of colleagues, or key pieces of information until you have committed them to memory. But if you do need to ask for help many times, nobody will think badly of you for doing so. Above all, do not panic, and do not make the mistake of taking your own assessment of your performance too personally, that is, keep in mind that you will improve over time, that everyone feels somewhat out of their depth at first in a new situation, and that as you come to master the tasks set before you, you will be able to draw on your particular skills and personal attributes in making your individual contribution to the job. If you expect and accept that the work placement will present you with a personal challenge, you are less likely to become upset by perceived problems with your level of competence during the initial stages.

▶ Interpersonal concerns in the workplace

Workplace etiquette and procedure may give rise to problems particularly for students who have no previous experience of a similar environment. As I outlined in Chapter 5, the smooth running of the workplace is underpinned by a network of unwritten rules, so it is unsurprising that it takes time for a newcomer to assimilate the situation and integrate into it. It is important to be attuned to the workplace hierarchy which involves being aware of who reports to whom, and to know who is responsible for certain functions. Without this knowledge it is difficult to find a niche within the overall team without inadvertently encroaching on territory that others may feel belongs to them. Moreover, if you are to make a valuable contribution, it is important to identify where your talents can best be directed.

In addition to these concerns, there is a myriad of unwritten guidelines relating to interpersonal issues, and since these are frequently far from tenuous it is easy to make mistakes. Within the workplace, individuals will have a strong sense of their own position and niche, and may expect others to acknowledge this, for example, by addressing them in a particular way, or by the level of formality or informality that is expected in any interaction. This is, of course, complicated by the fact that all personalities are different and a senior official in one organisation may well have a completely different outlook and strategy for running his or her team than a person at a similar level elsewhere. Also, whilst some people may expect to be treated as they treat others, it would be incorrect to assume that this is always the case.

Being included

Organisations vary as to the degree of informal conversation that permeates work discourse and the extent to which home life interacts with work. In some cases, staff play an important part in each other's personal lives. However, the spectrum is very broad and as a newcomer it is very, very difficult to determine what is considered to be appropriate behaviour and the timescale before which addressing colleagues in an informal and friendly manner might be considered by them to be 'forward'. This frequently gives rise to difficulties. Staff may not wish to include a newcomer immediately and may feel that attempts on the part of the student to be friendly are intrusive and unwelcome. Students may therefore feel excluded and isolated, particularly at times when the common ground established by work issues is not dominant, for example in the lunch break.

Being valued

Another area in which the reality tends not to live up to expectation centres on the attitude of other members of staff. Frequently, students find the transition from being an important individual within a defined academic group to a somewhat anonymous person in an unfamiliar landscape difficult, most particularly because for the first time they may encounter indifference on a large scale. Whereas at the start of a university module everyone is in the same position of requiring a great deal of guidance, in the workplace some staff will be more familiar and comfortable with the procedures to be followed than others, and all will be in a firmer position than a newcomer on work placement, who may therefore feel inadequate and isolated. Also, at university many students have left home for the first time and are keen to widen their circle of friends, but this is not necessarily the case in the workplace. A student on work placement may therefore find that, in the nicest possible way, they are totally ignored by everyone unless they make the approaches, and that they are excluded from any social arrangements. Moreover, whereas in a seminar or tutorial the value of any contribution they might make is applauded, the combination of being new, not being acquainted with the work or company procedure or any of the staff might mean that a student on work placement feels unable to demonstrate or prove value, and consequently is at first denied the self-satisfaction derived from respect and praise from others.

Personality issues

Individuals have their own way of working and students may be assigned to staff who feel that a student is a burden on their time. Far from making use of the student's talents and investing time in teaching them to be specifically useful for the job in question, they may side-step the issue and only hand over mundane and repetitive tasks. Clearly, this is problematic for the student concerned who may feel that he or she is being treated like a skivvy. Some employers may try to take advantage of work placement students by asking them to do more and more work and by extending their hours in the workplace. Students may feel intimidated by this, but may believe that they are not in a position to refuse. Worse still are situations that arise if a staff member has negative feelings about students in general, perhaps because in many organisations there is a graduate fast track to promotion that does not apply to other members of the workforce. In this situation a student may have to work alongside someone whom they feel does not like or respect them despite not having given them a fair chance, and this may be intimidating. Whereas, within the university situation, a student may expect to be treated with respect, this is not always the case in the workplace. And this is a two-way potential problem in that a student may find herself working for someone for whom she has little regard or respect. It is difficult to take instructions from somebody whom you feel is not handling a task or project well, but there may be little choice, and it is important always to behave in a polite and professional manner and keep such feelings private if your suggestions are clearly not welcome. For some students, this may be the first time they have encountered such a situation.

Whilst some staff members display great generosity to students in terms of offering their time to explain the workings of the department and being available to give direction if necessary, on other occasions students may just be given a task and left to do it without further explanation. With no direction and no feedback, the student can then never be sure whether progress is being made or how he or she might improve. Students who are used to regular meetings with their college tutor may find this particularly difficult. In the worst case scenario, students may be given the most unfulfilling jobs, excluded from team assignments and left to work without supervision or guidelines for long periods of time. Under such circumstances the student is likely to feel that he or she is not learning anything useful or contributing anything of value.

It is sometimes very difficult not to be affected personally when problems are encountered during a work placement. Whilst a good placement experience can result in increased self-confidence and self-esteem and a host of other bonuses, a bad experience can generate intense negative feelings. Emotions cited by students as a result of problematic placements include: anger; rebelliousness; intimidation; lack of confidence; loneliness; isolation; loss of self-esteem; stress; inability to cope; irritation; guilt; embarrassment and humiliation. Students experiencing one or more of these feelings are unfortunately by no means alone. If no action is taken, these feelings tend to fester and intensify, so it is important to address the situation and to try to change it. Later in this chapter, I shall offer guidelines on how this might be achieved.

▶ Practical issues

Financial
Although some work placements are paid, others are not, and even if travelling expenses are reimbursed in the latter case, over time the student may find that financial problems mar the benefits derived from the situation. There may be unforeseen additional expenses, such as the costs associated with accepting invitations to join work colleagues for lunch or for a drink after work. It may be embarrassing not to accept, yet the student may simply not be able to afford it. Moreover, the placement may prove to be very tiring and time-consuming, so for students who combine academic study with paid regular, casual work it may be more difficult to keep up all normal commitments and the result may be an overall drop in income.

Lifestyle concerns
The logistics of your day-to-day life during your work placement may give rise to problems. It may take up more time than you anticipated, either because the hours are longer or simply because you find that you need to give some time to thinking about the next day's tasks on the previous evening, or to devote some time to making notes for your learning log and reflective essay while the events of the day are fresh in your mind. Moreover, travelling may be more arduous and time-consuming than anticipated, or you may have to deal with unexpected personal or study-related problems the solutions to which have to integrate smoothly with your

work placement arrangements. You may, for example, find it more difficult than you had anticipated to keep on top of your university commitments and assignments, particularly if you are tired.

▶ Coping strategies and remedial guidelines

If you encounter problems of any nature with your work placement, it is vital that you address them rather than allowing the situation to intensify and become worse. If you take action, you will feel better for assuming control of the situation. This is clearly preferable to turning negative emotions in on yourself and remaining unhappy. However, you may also find it helpful to keep in mind that the primary reason for undertaking a placement is to broaden your experience and that, even if things go wrong, the experience will be useful to you as you embark upon your career post graduation.

▶ Preventing problems

This chapter has shown that most work placement problems stem from unfulfilled expectations. Therefore, the optimum strategy for avoiding problems in the first place is to identify expectations, particularly those relating to the nature and level of the work, competence in handling the workload and chances of integration within the workplace, and to evaluate the extent to which these are realistic. You may find it helpful to think of these issues from the perspective of the employer (see Chapter 7) and imagine what his or her expectations might be too. Any major discrepancy is likely to lead to problems. If you have difficulty in assessing your expectations, you might find it helpful to discuss them with your tutor, colleagues or friends.

If you are not clear about your work duties, contact your employer *before* the placement begins, as it is far easier to comment on and amend a hypothetical schedule than to become entrenched in a situation with which you are uncomfortable. If possible, ask for an outline of what you will be doing in writing because, if thought is given to your placement prior to your arrival, you are less likely simply to be faced with endless filing or equivalent tasks. Establish lines of communication and keep them open, for example, ask for the name of the person to whom you should report, Give this to your tutor and make sure that your employer has your tutor's details too. Sometimes it is more productive and less embarrassing if someone else negotiates on your behalf, so it is wise to organise a structure that can accommodate this before you start.

In terms of integration in the workplace, the best approach is to expect nothing! If you tackle your work in a professional way, you will be respected and accepted in due course, but the timescale is unpredictable so it is best not to count on anything. In the meantime, try to refrain from personalising issues and remember that if you are not included in office banter or invited to join your colleagues socially this is probably because they have known each other for some time and it is not something about which you should be unduly concerned.

▶ Strategies for improvement

The key point to remember about a work placement is that, whatever happens, it is a learning experience. This applies whether the work is fulfilling or disappointing, whether or not you become integrated as part of the organisation and regardless of the level of enjoyment you derive from the experience. You will learn simply by being in a workplace environment, putting your skills to practical use, observing others at work, taking instructions and reflecting upon your situation. However, if the placement is not proceeding according to your expectations, there are often measures that you can take to improve the situation.

Earlier in this chapter I emphasised the importance of clarifying the details of the placement prior to starting work, of identifying your mentor in the workplace and of ensuring that your tutor and mentor are in communication with each other. By taking these measures, you have ensured that the ground rules have been laid yet lines of communication remain open. Therefore if changes do need to be made, the procedure is relatively straightforward. During your placement, send your tutor regular updates so that if you are unable to resolve any problems yourself, your tutor is aware of the history. Above all, do not try to ignore problems.

Work-based issues

If the nature of the work is not what you anticipated, do not simply complain. Spend some time looking around you and try to find other work that you would prefer to do. You can then approach your employer with a reasoned argument as to why it might be beneficial to change. Show understanding for your employer's predicament with an assurance that you will finish the tasks in hand before moving on. If the entire work placement feels 'wrong', ask yourself what you were hoping to learn and try to identify how you might best achieve these goals within your current environment.

Even if shortly after starting your placement you realise that your future lies in another direction altogether, there will nevertheless be useful learning outcomes from your placement that will stand you in good stead in the future, albeit in a different sector.

If your workload is too heavy, keep a note of how you are spending your time and discuss this with your employer. Ask for assistance in prioritising tasks and check you are using the most time-efficient methods. You should not be spending too many extra hours in the workplace, and whilst it does not present a good impression if you watch the clock too closely, you should reasonably expect to leave the office within half an hour of your agreed time. If this is not the case you should discuss it with your employer. Similarly, if your workload is too light, or if you are engaged only in menial, repetitive tasks, try to identify work that you could do within the environment and volunteer for it. Students on work placement often benefit from discrete tasks that they can follow through from start to finish as this generates a sense of personal responsibility and job satisfaction. Whilst complaining is a negative action, making suggestions for improvement is positive! However, remember if you do have time between tasks that you can put this to good use by researching for your university presentation, and writing notes for your learning log and reflective essay. Alternatively, you can use the time to read promotional literature and general information about your placement organisation.

Interpersonal issues

If you encounter interpersonal difficulties, try not to take this to heart or let it upset you. If you keep a professional attitude at all times by maintaining an enthusiastic and hard-working attitude, accepting constructive criticism gracefully and trying to be as flexible as possible, then you will know that you have done your best. Remember that your aim is not necessarily to win your workmates' friendship, but to gain their respect.

Confrontation is best avoided as emotions can become over-heated and the outcome is usually more damaging than helpful. However, if you receive criticism that is personal and you are not sure how to deal with it, you have one of three options: You can do your best to ignore it, (whilst saving your opinions for your reflective essay!), and hope that the situation will resolve naturally; you can talk things through with your tutor and colleagues, or you can approach your employer. If you take the latter route, rather than simply complain, try to focus on the positive, for example, by stating briefly that the person concerned does not seem to require your services but that you have identified a need elsewhere and that you would be happy to transfer should they agree.

If you find that you are in an environment which is simply intolerable, for example if racism or sexism is considered acceptable, wait until you have gathered your thoughts and talk to your employer or your tutor. The law is on your side in such matters and your comments will be taken seriously.

Remember that there is something to be learnt from every situation. It may not seem directly relevant at the time, but everything you see, encounter and experience will add to your 'workplace skills' and stand you in good stead for the future.

▶ Summary

This chapter has focused on the most common problems faced by students on work placement. These may arise from the work itself, which may be inappropriate in terms of content, level or quantity, from interpersonal concerns within the workplace, or as a result of practical constraints such as limited finance or irreconcilable lifestyle issues. I have emphasised the need to think through expectations prior to starting a placement and suggested how problems may best be approached, analysed and dealt with. Offering alternatives is a good strategy for replacing a disappointing situation with a fulfilling one, and the fundamental point to bear in mind is that a great deal can be learnt from work placements that are beset with problems as well as from those that run smoothly and conventionally.

Perspectives and Feedback

A common problem we experience with work experience students, is the attitude that they are 'better' than the job that they are being asked to do. What students have to realise is that being able to do the most menial tasks with a smile, is the best way to prove your dedication to a prospective employer. Those that whinge about making their 50th cup of tea for the day rarely get ahead. Another problem is tardiness! Its crucial to arrive on time for placements (or even early!) and it's always a good idea to stay until your line manager is ready to go.

Celia, *employer – TV production*

I try to instil within my students a realistic attitude towards placements. Some do believe that they will be offered management experience early on in and are disappointed in the type of work offered to them. They need to realise that they will often find themselves doing lowly tasks such as photocopying (I sometimes tell them how long I myself spend on such tasks!) and that it's up to them to make the most of their experience. If the work offered is not sufficiently challenging, I suggest that they look around for a small project that they can undertake – this will give them a focus and will demonstrate that they are a creative thinker who shows initiative. Basically students need to take responsibility for their own learning whilst on placement and should never turn down opportunities to develop – they should attend meetings if are invited and always engage fully with colleagues, on a professional and social basis if possible.

Naomi, *tutor*

I was quite excited before I started at the library, because I love books and it sounded quite interesting. But when I got there, half the things I was told I could do I wasn't allowed to do. It ended up as a lot of shelving (by alphabetical or Dewey decimal system) and tidying of shelves. I ended up being incredibly bored for a lot of the time. It was fairly useless. The best part was being allowed to borrow things from the library for free.

Annette, *student*

The attitude of students, especially those who are pre-Higher Education, towards work experience can be irritating to say the least. A very able but stroppy student once informed me that she wanted 'a really good placement', as if she had some special right to it! Students often inform you what they will *not* do, rather than discussing what they will do. But students do often get really excited about going on work experience and it's a great pity when employers let them down by not having a proper programme worked out or by not designating someone to look after them and give them the attention and help they need. Work experience can be a negative experience if neither employer not student has realistic expectations. I've known students who've expected that they would be given a real job, even though the placement might only be for two weeks. They complain at being given menial tasks like photocopying or working on reception. Employers, on the other hand, might expect to get students who will willingly take on the most boring jobs without complaint. Free labour, in other words. Work experience under these circumstances can be de-motivating for the student, who then has a jaundiced view of the world of work, and can lead employers to refuse further placements when students complain about the treatment they are getting.

Jenny, *tutor*

One of the 'common problems' we have with work placements is that they often don't meet the expectations of the students. Especially when working in a radio station many students think the job is going to quite glamorous whereas the reality is very different. There might be opportunities to do 'fun' things such as helping out with bands and sessions but the majority of jobs might appear mundane. That doesn't mean these tasks aren't important – an organisation could not operate without them being done but it is not the sort of job the students expect to be doing or would like to be doing. This is because expectations of employers and students often don't match up which is probably a communication problem. This should best be resolved by employers giving students a list of the tasks they will be expected to perform on work experience. In a highly-skilled environment such as our own we can't just let students loose but often we do not have the time to train the students – work experience should not be confused with work training. Many firms do not have work experience schemes as they see them as too time consuming.

Jeremy, *employer – radio*

I had to commute into London which meant early mornings and late nights. When you're not getting paid and sometimes being ignored, this could have got you down. Everyone was so busy, all the time, I sometimes felt I was a burden.

Kelly, *student*

People sometimes just leave and don't come back, probably because they think they are going to be art directing the magazine when they are on work placement and doing quite menial tasks. I think they need to understand what work is really like.

Amanda, *employer – magazine*

The most common problem I found was the overall poor quality of the boring, mundane tasks. I also found that students liked to show too much initiative too early in the placement, again resulting in poor results. Initiative is good but students need to learn the ropes before making suggestions to current procedures.

Alistair, *employer – marketing for new media*

I did feel a level of hostility from some people and others felt a need to exert authority over me. Some of the other employees only saw me as a work experience person. I was asked at one point to clean. This made me feel that I was only seen by some people as someone there to run around after them to make their job easier. I was not on this placement to clean. I therefore voiced my concern with my boss who told me that was not my job and I was here to work as part of a team. My boss really made me feel that I was equal in the workplace.

Anastasia, *student*

7 Understanding Employers' and Tutors' Perspectives

This chapter will:

▶ consider the employer's perspective, focusing on and explaining key concerns
▶ suggest ways of approaching reluctant employers
▶ examine the role of the work placement tutor and identify how students might make the most of this resource

The greater part of this book focuses on the experience of work placements from the point of view of the student. However, in order for students to have a complete understanding of the overall process and the various influences affecting each stage, it is useful to consider the opinions of the other relevant parties. It is very important for students to be aware of the employer's motivation and point of view since many problems with work placements stem from a mismatch of aims and expectations between students and employers. If students understand both what it is that employers want and the reasons behind any reservations employers may have, they are in a better position to overcome or avoid difficulties. Similarly, an understanding of the tutor's perspective enables the student to develop a relationship that works to maximum mutual advantage.

In Chapter 1 the key benefits of work placements to employers are outlined. In the best case scenario, an employer may take advantage of the talents, skills and fresh outlook offered by the student to supplement the existing workforce and tackle either a backlog or a current project efficiently and at little extra cost. With this template in mind, it is hardly surprising that many students believe they are doing employers a favour by offering their services and they are surprised to have their application rejected. However, for some employers, there is a downside that outweighs the potential advantages of a work placement, and for this reason they may be reluctant to accept a student. In the course of your applications for a placement, you are likely to encounter employers who hold these views and for this reason it is important to have an understanding of the employer's perspective. Hopefully, you will then be able to demonstrate that you have not only considered their concerns but that you are able to counter them with positive suggestions that will work well in the particular situation in question. Indeed, if you are targeting an organisation that rarely takes students, and you have an idea as to the reason why, it might be appropriate to address this issue in your initial letter of application and offer assurances as to why, in your case, the situation will be different.

▶ Understanding employers' concerns

Workplace issues
The main reason cited by employers for not wishing to take a work placement student is that the student would not be a useful addition to the workforce. By this they mean that the student would not be immediately useful and would not warrant the investment of time necessary to train them to make a valuable contribution. Moreover, some are concerned that far from easing the burden on other staff, a work placement student would make the situation worse as one member of staff would be required to leave his or her regular duties in order to be available to assist the student in acclimatising within the organisation.

Additional reasons given include the belief that there would not be sufficient work of the appropriate level to justify the use of another person, or that the available work would be too difficult to handle. Whilst there might well be low-level repetitive work such as filing, many employers consider that it would not be fair to take on a placement student simply to cover such a mundane task, or that even this type of work would be more efficiently done by someone with a basic knowledge of the business.

The bottom line is that if an employer does not believe that it would benefit the business to take on a work placement student, he or she is unlikely to be receptive to applications.

Interpersonal and attitudinal issues
You may well find that your problems are compounded by the employer's previous experiences or those of business colleagues. He or she may have taken on work placement students in the past and may have encountered problems as a result. You could also be fighting an imaginary demon in

that, with no evidence either way, the employer may simply think taking on a work placement student is more likely to be problematic than beneficial. Whilst the majority of work placements are successful for both parties, some are not, and typical criticisms of work placement students cited by employers cover a number of key areas.

Some employers take issue with the student's appearance and behaviour. Clearly, it is necessary to be dressed appropriately for the job in question and in many instances this calls for a smart appearance. Fashion items and informal clothing are therefore frowned upon in some organisations. Employers expect staff to be punctual and reliable and if a work placement student is unable to conform to this basic request, he or she is unlikely to impress the employer or be given any significant responsibility. It is also essential to be aware of company policy on, for example, reading and sending personal emails in the lunch hour, and making and receiving personal telephone calls at work, as failure to adhere to company policy will result in criticism. Whilst it is good if the student integrates well with other staff, employers obviously become irritated if the student tends to take too many breaks and engage other personnel in conversation for too much of the time as this is effectively preventing everyone from getting on with the work. Similarly, if the student appears not to be focused on the work in hand and is therefore slow in producing results, this may lead to problems as others may feel under greater pressure as a result. Employers like students to have the initiative to get on with work without too much direction and those who require constant supervision are likely to be more of a liability than a help. Also, it can upset the harmony of the office if staff are very busy and the student is apparently oblivious to this and constantly interrupts with his or her own concerns whilst simultaneously being unwilling or unable to offer assistance to others.

Students who complain to other staff about the organisation or the work they have been given create a poor impression of themselves and generate bad feeling. Moreover, they tend to achieve less than if they were to adopt a professional approach and speak politely to their line manager about any problems. Some of the worst complaints about students cited by employers are that they do not want to do the work that they have been given; that they do not want to work in the way that the employer has asked; that they believe they know best and act accordingly; that they are inflexible, uncommitted or unfocused; and that they are of the opinion that they are doing the employer a favour, particularly if they are unpaid, and therefore that their contribution is in a sense 'voluntary', whereas the employer believes that the student is being offered an experience comparable to an apprenticeship and is therefore in a sense being given 'free' training. Obviously these criticisms can be applied to all potential employees and not just work placement students, but the difference is that if an employer finds that a new full-time employee has serious difficulties with certain aspects of the work or with personal attitudes, time and training can often improve the situation. However, in the case of work placement students, there may not be the necessary time before the agreed period of work comes to an end, and therefore, employers have less incentive to invest time, effort and resources.

The objective of this chapter is not to imply that there are many problems for employers associated with work placement programmes. Far from it! Most placements run smoothly and both parties gain a great deal from the experience. However, work placements do not simply happen: the employer needs to be persuaded by the student that it is in his or her best interest to support the placement. If the student is aware of any preconceptions, misconceptions or even previous problems encountered by the employer, he or she should address these and present assurances as to why they would not reoccur, and give reasons why the placement would benefit the employer and the organisation in question.

▶ Suggestions

As I have mentioned in previous chapters, confirming the details of the work placement in writing prior to its commencement benefits both employer and student alike as it presents the opportunity for either side to notice flaws in the arrangements and to make improvements. This then reduces the likelihood of a mismatch of expectations between employer and student. I have also mentioned the value in opening lines of communication between the employer, the student and an intermediary, probably the work placement tutor. However, there are other measures that can also be taken.

Some of the most fulfilling work placements owe their success to the fact that, in addition to general duties, the student has been given a discrete project that is his or her own responsibility to see through to completion. This tends to lead to the situation where, after an initial period, the student is clear about what needs to be done and is able to use her or his skills to execute the project without constantly referring to others. This way of working allows the student to be creative and to make key decisions, and most importantly allows him or her to encounter many of the emotions that accompany long-term work through what is essentially a microcosm of the working experience. For example, in carrying out the project the student will be aware of whether it is going well or badly; whether more effort is required; whether more data need to be collected or more reflection is needed; and what it is like to work under time pressure. Hopefully, the project will become increasingly absorbing and reward the student finally with a strong sense of job satisfaction through the production of a piece of work of which the student may justly be proud. Moreover, there are other benefits associated with working on a discrete project, most particularly that it is easier to identify the individual's contribution. Also, as the student has seen the project through from beginning to end, he or she is likely to be able to speak about it in an articulate, confident and enthusiastic manner on future occasions, such as forthcoming job interviews.

With this in mind, it is in everyone's interest to locate discrete jobs that can be done by a work placement student. After only one interview, the student is probably not in a position to identify such tasks, so it would be beneficial to both parties to meet again prior to the placement. If the student is given a tour of the organisation or department and is given the opportunity to ask questions, it will be far easier for both parties to identify suitable opportunities. If this is not possible, another approach might be to give the student current literature about the organisation to see if this prompts any suitable suggestions. Having done this, a brief meeting between employer and student prior to the placement starting, with the purpose of reiterating what the student has to offer and what the employer needs, provides an ideal opportunity for any new ideas to come to the fore.

There is also a great deal that can be done to smooth the way for future work placement students in the same organisation. It is essential that the employer and the student give each other feedback following the work experience. This will not only enable the student to target specific areas for improvement, but will also help the employer to identify what worked well during the placement and what did not. Employers who offer ongoing placements for different students each year might consider producing a short handout containing basic information such as who does what, useful telephone numbers and where information may be found, as this will save time by ensuring that the student is provided with an immediate overview of the situation. Current work placement students might consider drafting or improving the handout as part of their work assignment.

▶ The work placement tutor

In this book I have made frequent references to the work placement tutor as he or she is a very valuable resource for students. However, in order to make best use of the tutor, it is useful for students to have some insight into the tutor's perspective: students need to know what they must do in order to put their tutor in the best position to support them.

Role of the tutor

Your tutor can help and advise you at each stage of the placement process. If you are clear about the sector in which you wish to work, your tutor can offer specific recommendations, and if you are unclear, he or she can help you identify what you are good at and what you enjoy, and can then make suggestions. You may reasonably expect help with each stage of the application process, from writing your CV and covering letter to attending the interview, and your tutor can check any details about which you may have concerns, for example the insurance situation. If you have problems during your placement, your tutor is the person to whom you should turn, and if you require advice regarding the written assignments required for the university, your work placement tutor should be in a position to offer help and clarification. The success of the relationship between tutor and student hinges on the tutor having an honest and truthful impression of the student's character; career preferences if any; skills; strengths; weaknesses; and progress in terms of applying for and attending the work placement.

Key benefits for the student

Clearly, if you make the most of what the tutor has to offer, as outlined above, this effectively means that you will have the benefit of a mentor at all stages of the work placement process. Moreover, in addition to this, your tutor may be invaluable in liaising between you and an employer at crucial times, not just if there are problems during the placement, but also before the placement starts. You may find that a reference from your tutor will cement a work placement for you because it may answer and dispel any reservations your employer may have had, or indeed it may confirm a positive impression you have made. Your tutor, as a respected member of the academic community who knows you well both in terms of your work capabilities and your personal attributes, can carry great weight when it comes to securing a work placement.

Problems facing tutors

In order to offer the best possible advice, your tutor needs to be aware of all the nuances of any given situation. There is nothing to be gained by misleading your tutor as this may result in inappropriate decisions being taken. Of all the criticisms cited by tutors, lack of communication is the most predominant. This usually manifests itself in a situation where the tutor is suddenly faced with a problem, having been given no previous indication that anything was wrong. This means that the tutor has generally had little or no time to consider the various options or to reflect upon the best course of action. Don't lose sight of the fact that your tutor is also the person to whom employers turn when things go wrong, and it is most unfair to expect your tutor to sort out a problem that has first been drawn to his attention by the employer.

How students can help

Students can help by being totally honest with the tutor at all stages of the work placement process. If you have relevant specific circumstances, for example, that you have family responsibilities at certain times of the day, mention this early on to the tutor as he or she is then forewarned and may take this into consideration when advising you about your placement. Do not fail to mention certain factors in the hope that somehow everything will work out for the best.

Try to get to know your tutor as this makes it easier for her to ascertain the right course of action for you. Send regular feedback! This may take the form of a very brief email from time to time or longer correspondence when necessary. Even if everything is going well, keep in touch with your tutor, as otherwise it may not be clear what is happening and whether or not you need assistance. In the event of a problem with your employer, make sure that your tutor is aware of your side of the story before (s)he is called upon to respond to the employer.

If you suddenly decide to opt out of an arranged placement, let your tutor know as soon as possible so that you can discuss the best course of action. Remember that your tutor is likely to approach employers each year and ask them to take students, and if you change your mind about a placement and do not inform the employer in an appropriate manner, you are not only affecting your own placement but possibly souring a relationship between your tutor and the employer which may have repercussions for future students.

What if there is no tutor?

Some individuals will not have a tutor. If this is the case, it is doubly important to try to ensure that there are no misunderstandings between you and your employer. Do not leave anything to chance, or memory, but rather confirm all arrangements in writing. Try to think ahead and if possible establish regular feedback sessions between you and your employer from the outset. Also, ensure that there is a third party to whom you may turn for advice. It is not unreasonable to ask your employer to designate a 'line manager' or equivalent with whom you may communicate. A tutor would have enabled you to talk through your observations and thoughts and (s)he could potentially have helped in dealing with problems. In the absence of a tutor, it is wise to recruit friends and peers with whom you can discuss your experiences and establish a third party to whom you may turn in the event of problems in the workplace.

▶ Board of studies/programme board

Prior to a work placement module being introduced as part of the syllabus, a draft of key aspects of the course, normally written by the academics intending to oversee it, is sent for approval to the Board of Studies. The document provides information on all aspects of the module, including the delivery, management and organisation, rationale and learning outcomes and assessment requirements and guidelines. The final documentation may therefore be a useful resource for some students who wish to look very closely at the components and requirements of the module, although for many, discussions with their tutor will suffice. However, some students, for example, find it helpful to keep a list of the learning outcomes to hand whilst they are drafting the content of their reflective essay. If you do require a copy of this, the administrator in your departmental office is likely to be able to locate it for you.

▶ Summary

This chapter has focused mainly on the employer's perspective, noting that some employers are reluctant to take on work placement students. This may be because they feel that the time investment they would have to make in training the student cannot be justified in terms of the return, because they do not consider that they can offer suitable work, or because they fear that a student with an inappropriate attitude would bring problems rather than benefits. Such views may have arisen as a result of disappointing experiences in the past. It is very important for students to understand these key concerns in order to consider how best to counter them and convince the employer of their value to the organisation. Some suggestions as to how to do this are outlined, for example by using a tutor's reference to allay specific anxieties. This chapter also highlights some key concerns expressed by tutors, since if students are aware of these and adapt their behaviour accordingly, they will be able to make the most of this valuable resource and derive the greatest benefit from their tutor's expertise. It also makes recommendations for individuals on work experience who do not have a tutor.

Perspectives and Feedback

One student I knew went to a really good and well-known xxx company for his work experience, but when he returned complained that for a good deal of it he had just been on reception fielding phone calls and greeting visitors. I talked this through with him and tried to get him to see that this had been valuable for him. First of all, the company had put him in a position of great trust as the first contact with outsiders and secondly he gained lots of experience of dealing with people and thirdly, by keeping his eyes and ears open, he had found out a lot about how the company worked. I think that students, even older ones, get more out of work experience when their tutor can talk things through with them. It's too late once the placement is over – this is just one way in which visits during placements are so important. Students who dislike their work placements will sometimes absent themselves. Now, if they've been in touch with their tutor to say that they're unhappy, then at least the tutor can attempt to do something to improve the situation. But often students are embarrassed or apathetic and they find it easier to just not turn up. Then that sours the placement for future use. Tutors should train students to communicate with them – it's an important lesson for the future as well.

Jenny, *tutor*

My company took on many work placement students and my impression was that most of them were not interested in a career in a similar environment, but because careers staff found it difficult to find placements, students were not always given the opportunity to gain experience in their first or even second choice of career, the belief being any work experience is better than none.

Delia, *employer – insurance*

To me a work placement is about learning on the job so I prefer the old fashioned word apprentice. It does, of course, involve observing and listening, but most importantly it is about doing. It is only by doing that an apprentice is given the opportunity to learn, make mistakes, learn and grow in confidence. It can only be of benefit to both parties if the apprenticeship is one lasting more than a couple of weeks. It is important for the employer to feel that they have the time to spend and invest in a person – this can't be done in a short space of time.

Lesley, *employer – theatre*

I was involved with placing students in television and film production companies. It is quite difficult to explain the reality of this work whilst students are in a college context. There was always a risk of a student insisting on working strictly 9–5, or less, and being sent home. In one case I had impressed this so forcefully to a student on work experience at xxx [production company] that they had to send him home when it got past 21:00. We were both worried that he has overdone it but he got very good references and is still working in broadcasting.

Trevor, *tutor*

Placements vary enormously in length and scope. It is important that students have realistic expectations of themselves and the placement. It takes time to learn about an organisation and to pick up anything but the simplest of jobs. For shorter term placements, students may have a specific objective or responsibilities but these may not take up all of your time. If this is the case, you should aim to get the most out of the opportunity by observing and helping out with whatever is going on.

Caroline, *employer – human resources*

I feel that next year when I set up the placements I will insist on meeting the employer before the start of the placement to absolutely clarify what it is the employer has in mind for the student to do. It may be that the employer does not have anything in mind, in which case a visit to help with ideas of projects or to just talk things through, will be advantageous to everybody concerned. It has been no surprise that the most successful placements this year have been where the employer has thought out beforehand what the student will be doing. Where employers have a specific project or job in mind, I want to discuss it with the employer to make sure that it is manageable for the student, both for the time designated and the actual work involved. Visiting the students whilst they are on placement is very important. It makes them feel appreciated and allows the co-ordinator to get a realistic feel on how the placement is progressing, from the student's and employer's perspective. Visiting builds up rapport with the employer and helps them feel valued for all the work they are putting into the student.

Clare, *tutor*

I do however think students can get a lot of benefit by working in an organisation such as our own – even if it does not seem very hands on.

We make sure students work across all departments and it certainly gives them a good idea of what it is like to work in an office environment, of how to work within time deadlines and of how to interact with other colleagues. Equally organisations benefit because they have a keen voluntary workforce only too eager to please.

Jeremy, *employer – radio*

If the student doesn't understand the employer's perspective then it is entirely the fault of the employer. When a placement student joined our company they went through similar training to that of our sales people. That way they understood our goals and objectives before conducting any marketing task.

Alistair, *employer – marketing for new media*

Somebody new is always of interest and use in an office if they can offer a new skill, perspective or some unusual experience. Employers need and want new, enthusiastic staff but employers are generally older and therefore live different lifestyles than younger, placement students. They are therefore less tolerant or interested in staff coming in late though oversleeping or arriving with whopping hangovers. If a member of staff does more than they are asked to do, they are of benefit and generate respect and gratitude. If a new member does only what is required and acts as if the employers 'owes' them in terms of training, responsibility or payment, there's going to be trouble. Don't burn bridges or do 'home truths', either as an employee or employer. Most industries are quite small and word-of-mouth is immensely damaging, not to mention the fact that both parties will inevitably bump into each other again in months or years to come!

Michael, *employer – conferences and exhibitions*

8 Successes – Case Studies

This chapter outlines and describes the positive work placement experiences of four students. Benefits gained from the placements include:

- ▶ improvements in skills and employability
- ▶ increased self-confidence and self-awareness
- ▶ the confirmation of existing career ambitions or the introduction of new options
- ▶ the ability to assimilate all the opportunities offered by work-based learning

For these students, the placement has gone a considerable way towards easing the transition to the world of work.

▶ Mutiat

Mutiat undertook her work placement in her second year at university, at the age of twenty. She accepted unpaid work in theatre administration, eventually coordinating the arrangements for a community play scheduled to be performed in a new theatre still under construction at the time her placement began. Her commitment involved working one day per week for a minimum of ten weeks, based in an office opposite the theatre site, but in fact Mutiat volunteered to continue for several months because she did not want to leave with her work incomplete. She had originally sought a placement in a theatre as this was in keeping with her long-term career ambitions:

> The reasons I applied to a theatre to carry out my placement was because I have a great interest in theatre work and have extensive experience working on productions, mainly on stage. I'm also studying drama and theatre studies with cultural studies. In cultural studies we analyse society and look at institutions

like the Arts Council and areas of funding so I felt having a placement in the
theatre would complement both my subjects. Another reason I applied to the
theatre was because, as most of my theatre experience came from being on
stage, I felt that it would be a great opportunity for me to see how the theatre
worked backstage and behind the scenes.

Prior to Mutiat's arrival, it had been decided that a community play would
be a good way of involving those who lived and worked in the local
community in the new building and emphasising that the theatre could
become part of their lives. The play was also perceived as an opportunity to
raise awareness of the new theatre more generally. The response from the
public was considerable, with large numbers of people sending in CVs and
letters and offering to help with the production. Since there was no official
coordinator, Mutiat was given the job, having spent a few weeks acquainting
herself with the general running of the office by that time:

> After being assigned to be the co-ordinator, my job role meant I had to organise
> the CVs and letters from the people who wanted to be involved in the community
> play, organise and attend meetings. I also had to prepare professional actors
> who we used to demonstrate various scenes from the play to give participants
> an idea of what they were getting in to. I obtained music books for the
> Musical Director, proof read the script for the writer, obtained information on
> Performance Rights, as the play was a musical. I constructed a master schedule,
> rehearsal schedule, contact list and a feature cast contact list. I answered the
> telephone, took messages, called people, did photocopying and filing, obtained
> a first aid kit, as the play included many children, I organised auditions, organised
> rehearsal space, in person, by letter, and by telephone and gathered the logos
> from the companies that gave us money to fund the play. I used the computer
> and I marketed the play to companies in order to convince them to advertise in
> the community play's programme.

Before starting the placement, Mutiat had anticipated that as a student she
would be given very insignificant tasks to do, so she was surprised and
grateful to be given such stimulating work. She also thought that her previous experience in the theatre would enable her to cope very easily.
However, she admits now that her preconceptions were incorrect, mainly
because she was treated as a fellow professional by her colleagues from
the outset and was expected to act on her own initiative and work hard.

Mutiat did encounter some problems whilst on work placement, but
was able to find her own solution to these issues. The first was when
the administrator decided to appoint a project manager as Mutiat's availability was not sufficient to cover the busy audition and rehearsal schedule.

She notes that:

> This also caused a few problems as I was used to working in my own style but this had to change and I felt my role was being taken over by the project manager. I realised this wasn't the case as there were other aspects of the community play that needed attention, so I decided to focus on getting advertisers for the community play's programme, while the project manager focused on the participants' organisation.

There were also practical problems, most particularly arising from the timings of rehearsals, which ended very late. As Mutiat had to travel for over an hour to get home she felt that it was unrealistic and also unsafe to attend meetings that ended around ten o'clock at night. However, she was able to come to a very amicable arrangement with the project manager by offering to attend more of the daytime rehearsals plus the first hour of evening rehearsals in order to take registers and note the names of those who did not attend. She observes that: 'This meant that we both worked together on the community play but didn't get in each other's way.' Indeed, Mutiat's approach was to envisage herself as part of the team and to try to alleviate the workload of her colleagues whenever possible.

> I helped the process of theatre production to run smoothly. Everyone was informed of what was going on through my contact lists and felt they could contact me for information. It made me feel useful and trusted. By organising rehearsal space it meant that that was one less area for the director to think about. I made sure no one worried about particular areas of the production because I made sure those areas were tackled and completed. I took workloads off other people's backs, by helping out with smaller areas like filing and telephoning, I allowed others to focus on more important aspects while I focused on making sure things were ready for the following week.

Through her work placement, Mutiat felt that she gained insight into the different yet interlinked contributions made to a production by the administration, finance and marketing departments, and overall she witnessed the importance of teamwork. She also learnt that 'the sector is one that relies on persistence', citing her observations of staff in the finance department who repeatedly had requests for funding turned down and who then had to think of different organisations they might target. The need for patience in organising meetings around many different schedules also came as something of a revelation. Mutiat is able to summarise her learning outcomes as follows:

> I've learnt a great deal in this placement. I've learnt to overcome problems and
> to not be stressed out by them and to be able to find a compromising solution.
> I've learnt to prioritise and to work in a team. As a co-ordinator I had to learn to
> work under my own initiative, to manage, but at the same time I was still
> learning from my administrator. I've learnt to organise on such a large-scale
> production, to retain a good memory, to be good at marketing and promotion, to
> have good presentation and communication skills, in person and on the tele-
> phone. I also learned a lot financially and I gained a lot of IT experience. The
> biggest learning achievement for me would be organisational skills.

Overall, Mutiat found the workplace environment friendly and stimulating,
and her output raised her self-esteem and gave her a sense of achievement.
She felt that others viewed her in a professional light, and she also gained
satisfaction from realising that her work was appreciated. The experience
was not only rewarding, but also useful in terms of helping Mutiat to make
decisions about her future:

> Working with the theatre has allowed me to realise, through my adaptability,
> that there are many aspects of the theatre world that I can enter. Also, it has
> made me see that I really do prefer acting than being a coordinator. I think this
> realisation was emphasised when I was watching the actors rehearse. I felt a
> need to be part of the acting group. I've learnt a great deal in this placement. I've
> learnt to overcome problems and to not be stressed out by them and to be able
> to find a compromising solution. I've learnt to prioritise and work in a team.

This positive view was shared by her employer who noted that as the
weeks progressed Mutiat's self-confidence increased. This was particularly
noticeable in terms of the skills she demonstrated in coordinating significant numbers of participants over the telephone. She observes that:

> Mutiat's shy and retiring manner soon gave way to an abundance of energy and
> new found confidence. This growing confidence was demonstrated in her ability
> to tackle her dedicated tasks with more and more initiative as the placement
> progressed. She was a quiet, determined learner who understood the value of
> undertaking a placement – that is what she could both gain and give in return.

▶ Thomas

Thomas is twenty-two years old and is currently in his final year as an
economics undergraduate, having spent last year on work placement at a

leading accountancy firm. When choosing his university, Thomas specifically focused on those offering work placements and finally opted for a thick sandwich course – two years at university followed by a year in industry and a final year at university. He believed that a work placement would significantly improve his chances of securing employment after graduation.

Although Thomas's university offered substantial support in finding a work placement, he secured his own by searching for opportunities on the Internet and then making an online application. He targeted large organisations that offered graduate training schemes and were prepared to make these accessible to work placement students wishing to work for one year only. Having identified a suitable opportunity, the next step was to complete the online application form. Thomas noted that: 'They have seventeen or so applications per place, so they can't interview all of these as much as they may like to' and concluded that: 'It's all about the form.' He spent longer than the suggested time on his application form, and, realising that most applicants would have good academic credentials, he emphasised his extra-curricular achievements and interpersonal skills:

> I told them about things I'd done, for example my gap year. I took a gap year out and travelled around the world, which meant organising that, planning it, and obviously being there to change plans when things went wrong. Also I'd been a chairman of a society at university. And I'd also been the representative on the student–staff liaison committee in my department, and am currently the faculty rep. I was also elected to congress in the student union. Looking at the people I worked with there were some similarities. Everyone seemed to have been a chairman of a society or a sports club, a captain of a sports club, or somewhere down the ranks. One would not necessarily have to be the Chairman but could be the vice-Chairman – everything is relative. But in general most of them had a position of leadership, of responsibility, somewhere where they could use communication skills and ensure that they were good at it.

After an interview with a Senior Manager and having sat a series of psychometric tests, Thomas was invited back a week later to an Assessment Centre. On this occasion, he was interviewed by a Senior Partner and took part in assessed group exercises. Shortly afterwards he was advised that his application had been successful. The scheme offered by his organisation was a very structured one, and Thomas, like the other work placement students and graduate trainees, was expected to study for and take two accountancy exams in the first few months. There were also other benefits in working for a large organisation in that it had worldwide business interests and connections together with a generous budget for staff training and development. It was also accepted that there was a significant likelihood of future opportunities for work placement students within the organisation if the original agreement between the two parties worked well. Thomas took full advantage of all these possibilities. Having passed his first two accounting exams, he 'made it known that I would be happy to do the next four', which he subsequently passed. He also asked to visit the organisation's Moscow office, as this was where he hoped to work after graduation. Thomas notes that there are abundant opportunities within a worldwide organisation of this calibre but there is nevertheless no absolute guarantee of work at the end of the placement and it is up to the individual to carve out his or her own career path:

> They are not spoonfeeding you. It is not school. It's the survival of the fittest in some respects. It is a meritocracy. They do push you to an extent. Everything is within time lines etc. You've got exams you have to do by this date and on that date. You've got things they expect you to do on an annual basis. They expect you by year two to have got to this level. But other than that, you have got to get yourself there.

In his own case, Thomas 'felt by passing my first two exams that I have shown I've got the necessary skills to continue doing the exams. That's what they look for. It's rather like a first hurdle.' After the second phase of exams he requested to sit for the third phase at which point he was asked whether or not he intended to come back as a member of staff after graduation. Since this was his intention and ambition, the organisation enabled him to sit a total of ten accounting examinations whilst on work placement with them.

Thomas very much enjoyed the workplace culture. The company organised several social evenings to bring together permanent members of staff, graduate trainees and work placement students. They also financed various group visits away from the office, with the purpose of developing and honing communication and inter-personal skills. Thomas's group chose to go to Brussels and he has clear memories of the team-building day which took the form of a treasure hunt with various groups being given cameras and a brief to photograph particular items. Thomas recalls that:

> It was absolutely brilliant because it's a really good way to team build and to spend time with people, and to get to know people better whereas you wouldn't do that in an office environment.

Thomas was very happy with the terms and conditions of his work placement. He was paid as a graduate trainee and was given similar work, the majority of which tested his skills thoroughly. Very, very occasionally his work involved 'less complex' tasks, and then Thomas did 'what I thought was necessary to get a larger job done', pragmatically noting:

> That's just the nature of the job. I'm doing half an hour of photocopying which needs to be done and that's fine. Either I do it or someone who is getting paid twice the amount that I do [does it]. I got paid the same as a graduate, so I was very, very happy doing whatever a graduate did. And I did do the same as a graduate. I had the same level of responsibility.

During his work placement, Thomas's tutor visited him twice, and in addition, there were two separate days on which all work placement students returned to the university to share experiences and information. Thomas felt that as his placement scheme was a very structured one, with few surprises, this support service was less essential for him than for others whose placement may not have lived up to expectations.

Thomas is currently part of the way through his final year at university. He will be returning to his placement organisation as a full-time member of staff after graduation, but in the meantime he keeps in constant contact. The company has already outlined the job package they would like to offer him after graduation and he visits from time to time. On the last occasion, he attended an evening organised by the company for potential employees and spoke to them about his own experiences. For Thomas, the work placement has not only established a bridge between university study and employment; it has also enabled him to attain qualifications and experience that ensure a head start in his chosen career:

> The 'insider knowledge' is priceless – once you can 'speak' the industry language then you can get your foot in many doors (whereas a graduate without experience may not understand quite what they are looking for). You are a safer bet for the company, and a better investment too. [And on a more personal note] I made some of my best friends through my placement – friends for life!

▶ Nicky

Nicky is sixteen, and 'really didn't have any idea at all' about where she wanted to undertake her two-week work placement at the end of year eleven. Having made some general enquiries she opted for a placement in the buying and merchandising section of a major department store which she secured via a neighbour who worked there. Two places were available so Nicky attended with a friend. Originally the idea was for one person to be seconded in the first week to the swimwear department and the other to the handbag department, with a view to changing in the second week. However, it was later decided that they could be more productive working together.

Before arriving at the store, Nicky did not know what to expect. Indeed, she recalls that 'we were quite worried we were going to be doing photocopying and things like that.' However, the department had organised a schedule, which was given to the girls on the first day: 'They set out a sheet for us telling us what we would be doing. It was varied. They gave us lots of different things.'

On the first day they were given the task of 'comp shopping' which required them to look at the products available in other stores and make discrete notes. Another employee showed them the basics, but then they were left to undertake the task unsupervised.

> You can't do comp shopping on your own. You have to go into all the other businesses and see how they set out their products for example, the layout of the swimwear, what brands they have, their prices, for example on their mix and match bottoms and tops, the range of prints they have, and any special offers. One of us would write and the other would quietly tell them. You had to look like you were shopping because [otherwise] you can get thrown out.

Having gathered the data, the girls then input it into a spreadsheet. They were given basic guidance but were encouraged to devise their own headings and structure. Another employee checked that they were coping with the work and on the first day they were taken to lunch. Comp shopping became a regular task during the placement, and the girls were given feedback which enabled them to improve their methods to match what was required:

> They told us how we could have improved our spreadsheet and they said it was good and we had got everything down that we needed to. They had set out their sheet in a more logical way than we had and we had written great big chunks about everything. We had described every bit of swimwear in every shop. And they said: 'You don't need to do that. You just need to say there are this many patterned ones, this many plain ones ...'

Other tasks included shadowing the designers to witness at first hand what the job entailed, and practical tasks such as taking photographs of swimwear on a mannequin. This involved photographing the mannequin in a variety of outfits using a digital camera. The photographs were then sent to the Head of Buying to illustrate what was planned for the following year. Nicky felt that she and her colleague were able to make a valuable contribution to the work of the department by doing this task well:

> We did that in a pair so that they could just leave us to do that. It takes them a long time especially as one of them is normally doing it by themselves. Whereas one could put the swimming costume on and one could take the picture and then we could switch it quicker, so it was definitely easier.

The store also capitalised on the fact that the two girls were in the same age group as their target shoppers and gave them tasks that would inform the permanent staff and assist them with buying decisions:

> They sent us out one day with £20 to buy some beachwear accessories because that's what they are going to be going into next year. They've never done it before so they said: 'You will be the age group that's buying it and we want to see what you think.' We went to H & M because they were good for cheap accessories and we bought bracelets made out of shell and we bought some plastic bangles that matched some of the swimwear that we had seen before and flowers for your hair and things like that. And we went toTopshop and New Look and we went all around. That took us about two and a half hours. We then told them why we had chosen them and what we liked about them and why we thought they would sell. And they used some of our ideas and they were using one of the colours that we had found with their style of flower, so it was going to be hot pink instead of the duller pink that they had already picked out. And then we got to go to a meeting with their suppliers who they were just about to start up a relationship with. And they liked our ideas and what we were doing. It was good to see how they were presenting them.

Nicky felt that she was treated well by everyone with whom she had contact at the department store. Although the placement was unpaid, travelling expenses were reimbursed and she was given a small allowance that covered the cost of lunch in the subsidised canteen. Most of the other staff worked through their lunch hours with a sandwich at their desks, but care was taken to ensure that she always had an appropriate break. The girls got on very well with the other staff and were taken out to lunch at a local restaurant on their last day. Nicky believes that she and her friend were treated 'more like equals' than students, citing the fact that 'they trusted our opinions and used some of our ideas'.

Prior to starting the placement Nicky had been advised to dress in smart casual clothing so she arrived on the first day wearing a skirt, a shirt and some smart shoes which were not in fact comfortable or suitable for comp shopping. Nicky noted that most of the other staff were wearing jeans, flip-flops and vest tops.

> I felt a bit uncomfortable and out of place [on the first day]. Some people like the head buyers were smart but they were all comfortable, whereas my shoes really hurt. And the girl we were with noticed that my feet were hurting and she said 'Oh you should have said. I'd have got you some flip-flops to wear.' So I felt a bit stupid then. The second day I went in in some normal trousers and a top and some comfortable trainers and it was much better.

Gradually, during the course of the placement, Nicky's confidence grew:

> Probably at the beginning I was quite nervous about giving my opinion. I said I liked everything, but as the week went on and I got to know the people more and I got more confidence I gave more opinions.

She was also encouraged by the enthusiasm of her colleagues for their work, which she found infectious. She noted that they would arrive early and leave late, and come in talking about ideas that had occurred to them overnight. Nicky 'was quite surprised that they all loved their jobs and it wasn't just one person it was all of them, the whole team. We were just as enthusiastic as they were which they were pleased about. They were really grateful.'

Overall, Nicky found her work placement experience very valuable. She did not have preconceived ideas about what to expect and was pleasantly surprised by the positive aspects of working as part of a team in retail buying. She particularly enjoyed getting involved in all aspects of the work of the department, sharing her views and listening to the opinions of those around her. She would now like to return to the store at some point in the future to expand her experience. Indeed, for Nicky, the work placement may turn out to be the first step in a career in retail buying:

> I've now got an idea of what I want to do. I would love to be a buyer for a big company like that. It's given me more idea of what I want to do at university as well – probably European Business Studies with Spanish, because I think that would help me.

▶ **Harry**

Harry is twenty-one years old and is studying for a degree in multi-media journalism. His obligation was to commit to six weeks of work placement experience during the first two years of his degree, and Harry decided early on that instead of aiming for six continuous weeks in one placement, he would prefer to gain a broad range of experiences from a spectrum of organisations specialising in both print and broadcast journalism. This means that now, in his third year, he is able to benefit from evaluating and comparing organisations and the experiences they offer the work placement student:

> I thought it was much more important to get a range of placements under my belt rather than one big one. So whereas some people did three weeks at one place I don't think that's the best way to do it. I would say go and get more placements and [aim for] a shorter amount of time. I think that's pretty much the key thing in my opinion. You are always going to be on work experience which means that if you can go for three days or three months you can pretty much get the same out of three days as you can from three months. Obviously you are not going to do as much but in terms of sampling what goes on there you can get a flavour of it in a week. You won't get much more responsibility after four weeks or four months because you are just a work experience boy. You will get more experience but you can't get any more responsibility. I think that really is the key thing.

All Harry's placements were unpaid and he found each of them without assistance from his university tutors. Initially, he approached the task of securing a placement by writing a 'hopeful letter' to several organisations. 'Probably from most places I didn't get a response back at all, but I knew that was going to happen anyway. My plan was to get one or two back. I must have sent off about twenty each time, and I couldn't believe how many I was getting back.' (Basically Harry wrote so many letters that although the take-up rate was low, he still managed to acquire a good number of offers.) In his first year Harry targeted newspapers and in his second year he targeted broadcasters. In all instances he wrote to a specific person in the sports department as sport was his particular area of interest:

> I was pretty honest – I just said I'd like to get a placement. I'd like to spend some time in your department which was true. I don't know if that came across because a lot of people write letters and don't mean it. I was really keen to go and sample it. I suggested a week or so. I made it sound minimal so they wouldn't read it and think – [oh no!] this kid wants to spend 6 weeks here! I think that helped. It probably helped that I was going to a department as opposed to a newspaper. The fact that I was keen on sport and applying to sports departments probably helped.

Harry was meticulous about doing his homework prior to applying for a placement. He found out the name and position of the person to whom he should write, and personalised his letter as much as possible:

> One thing that people always say is – just make sure that everything is well writ-
> ten. Some people just send of letters 'Dear Sir/Madam'. I wouldn't even dream
> of doing that. You have got to find out who you are writing to and address it to
> them and do a bit of homework. You can't just send off a token letter and expect
> to get lots in return.

Perhaps surprisingly, he was never invited for interview as a result of his
applications. He either received no reply, or was offered a placement. This
reinforced his conviction that the letter and CV were crucial. In each of
his first two years, Harry spent just under a month on work placement. His
individual assignments ranged from one day to over two weeks. The difference in the amount of time he spent with each organisation influenced
his contribution to the organisation concerned. On shorter placements he
tended to shadow staff, whereas on longer placements he was given
specific tasks and projects. The experience was also influenced by the size
and relative importance of the organisation concerned.

> It varied greatly. At some places I was very useful. At XXX in Birmingham I was
> quite important to them because they did not have the staff. I was going off and
> doing interviews for them and editing radio packages. I was doing stuff that was
> going to be broadcast, whereas at XXX nobody had any time for me at all,
> because it was such a busy place and it was such an important role they were
> doing. They were never going to give some kid the job of editing something that
> was going to be broadcast. That just wouldn't happen. I didn't do a lot there
> although it sounds good. It wasn't great. They [work placements] are certainly
> worthwhile. There is no two ways about it. They really are worthwhile but they
> do vary a great deal.

The consequence of such varied placements is that Harry made useful
contacts in some instances, whereas in other organisations he feels that
he did not make an impression and now feels that he could not contact
the same people for work in the future. His attitude whilst on placement
was 'to be confident' and 'not to shy away from anything. If you are asked
to do something – do it no matter what it is.' Harry recalls that on one
occasion nobody from the newspaper where he was on placement
was available to attend a book launch and cover it for the paper, so
although he was nervous he went along and did his best. This paid off as he
met not only the author of the book but also journalists from other organisations and was also able to practise his writing and interviewing skills.

Harry believes that:

> In a work placement person employers are looking for someone to be keen, willing to put themselves about and work hard and muck in. I think they would look for someone who is a good team player. That's a cliché but they would look for someone who gets on well with people. And I think confidence [is important]. They are not going to expect you to be a great journalist. And you're not. No one who goes on work placement is going to be a great journalist because that's just the nature of it – why would you be going on work placement? Because you need experience. But they'd look for you to be keen. Take your time, don't rush in and find you've made a massive mistake. If you do make a mistake then get on with it.

However, one formidable problem Harry faced was financing his various placements:

> I had to stay in university halls for the last two summers for three weeks at a time. It cost me £20 a night. It does cost a lot of money especially if you want to go to a place in London. You have to pay for transport. You have to pay for accommodation, especially if you don't know anyone. I didn't know anyone in London. I still don't. It's going to cost you a lot if you go to London but it's worth it.

Harry felt that he needed to work in London because in his first year he targeted national newspapers and in his second year he targeted major terrestrial broadcasters, many of whom were based there. Despite the cost, Harry believes that he has gained a great deal from his work placements. He notes that: 'My CV looks good now and when I came to uni it didn't. In fact it looked really quite bad. Most people on the course seemed to have some kind of experience already and I didn't have any. So I just decided I needed to sort it out.' The result is that 'I feel comfortable now, and confident that I could fit in anywhere. I could do a job.'

9 Disappointments – Case Studies

In this chapter four students share their disappointments about their work placements and explore the reasons for the underlying difficulties, which in several cases stemmed from the inappropriate nature, quantity and level of the work. These experiences also give valuable insight into the relationship between employer and student and highlight potentially problematic areas.

▶ Amelia

Amelia undertook a work placement in theatre administration in the second year of her degree course in Cultural Studies with Theatre Studies. Before going to university she had worked in treasury and banking, and at thirty she was slightly older than many of her undergraduate colleagues. Amelia decided to target a local theatre that had a good reputation for innovative work. Since she had previously worked there as a volunteer usher, she knew who to contact and was able to make her own work placement arrangements, namely to attend one day per week for a minimum of ten weeks. The work was unpaid, but she hoped, through her placement, to find out more about theatre administration and enhance her CV:

> I think it exposes you to an organisation that you would otherwise have no access to and it does make you open your eyes to it. Having worked in banking and then going into an arts organisation it's completely different. It opened my eyes to the question – is that what I really want to be doing at the end of the degree anyway? ... I think anything you can add to your CV is a bonus. Because if you are going in with nothing and you are competing with a lot of other people with nothing then how are they going to siphon out the good from the bad. And it also shows commitment I think.

As Amelia already knew her employer, the interview for her work placement was a formality, useful primarily to fix the dates in question. However, on that occasion her employer did not outline what the work placement would entail, and, with the benefit of hindsight, Amelia now recognises that this was a bad sign:

> This was part of the problem. I had to sit down and keep saying: 'Look I need to have something kind of physical – a structure – so that I can report it back.' But it was a case of – we can put you in the marketing department for a little while. We can put you in here. But when it came to the work placement it was literally – what can we do with her? And again I think that was a problem. So I did admin tasks and bits and pieces. I thought I would have a project or be used in a particular department for ten weeks. They didn't know what to do with me.

After a few weeks Amelia mentioned to her employer that she was particularly interested in cultural diversity. As a result of this conversation she was assigned to a specific research project with the purpose of inviting more culturally diverse theatre groups and organisations to the centre. However, even then there were problems, mainly because Amelia had practically no contact with the person in charge of the project as he was located elsewhere in the building and did not come in every day. Amelia notes that the workplace culture was 'very lax, or relaxed I suppose' (depending on one's perspective), but in her case she found the part-time working patterns of many employees together with the fact that an individual's schedule was often only known to the person concerned 'very frustrating'. She found that 'there was no bonding', whereas previously in her work in banking before university she had enjoyed interacting with colleagues and being part of a team. On her placement she was faced with the situation of arriving for work at the appointed time to find that no arrangements had been made for her. She then had to find a place to work whilst colleagues put their minds to an appropriate task for her. Amelia attributes this to a general lack of communication within the organisation but admits that she was partly to blame. She agrees that her employer and colleagues were probably unaware of her transferable skills and previous experience in finance and that she did not draw these to their attention. With hindsight she believes that regular feedback sessions would have helped, although she confesses to a reluctance to express disappointment with her placement to her employer at the time:

> I suppose it's a courtesy thing, which is ridiculous! I felt they were doing me a favour, as opposed to me doing them a favour. I should have done. [complained] In retrospect I should have done! Now I feel that it [my placement] was

irrelevant. The fact that I didn't take it as a credit – it was a waste of time. That was a real shame! Hang on, am I being too harsh? Was it a waste of time? It was interesting because I got to see how it worked. It wouldn't stop me going for a job in a similar role, but on a full-time basis. I think if it was a full-time job it would be completely different. If you were there five days a week then I'm sure it would. And if they were paying you a wage as well. There's much more accountability. Well I hope it would!

With the benefit of hindsight, Amelia now believes that everyone embarking upon a placement should meet their employer before starting work and discuss both the student's expectations and what the organisation can realistically offer, as 'then everyone knows where they stand'. She also points out that if students are offered two or three different placements this information can help to make the decision process easier. Amelia believes that it is important for students to consider the overall situation and question whether or not their expectations are too high. It is also essential to keep aims and objectives in mind:

> In a perfect world I think you go in with a list of objectives. I don't think I had any, and that's as much my fault as theirs. If I could turn the clock back I would have liked almost a mini-project, not in terms of a whole project but just – yes, these are your tasks and we want you to fulfil them by the end of your time. So in terms of objectives I'd know where I was going and I would give value back to the organisation. I think it's very important otherwise, which is what happened with me, I came away thinking: 'What was the point of that?' And I'm sure they thought the same, so it was a kind of lose/lose situation.

Amelia's experiences left her feeling that she was wasting her time at the theatre and that the circumstances prevented her from offering her employer anything of value. As a result she decided to withdraw from the work placement module. However, her conscientious and professional personality directed her to fulfil all her commitments at the theatre in terms of attending for work when she had offered her services, and indeed, her tutor received a good report from her employer. However, Amelia felt that she had not made enough of a contribution to generate sufficient data for the university assignments she would need to submit in order to pass the work placement module:

> When I finished the placement I didn't feel that I had enough work to put into it, and I knew if I submitted anything I wouldn't get a good enough grade, and at the end of the day what I wanted was a good grade. I didn't have enough meat for the bones. I didn't feel that I had any end result, anything tangible.

Amelia went on to graduate successfully. She is currently working in banking again, but continues to search actively for opportunities in keeping with her long-term career ambitions in arts administration.

> When you go into a different sector you don't know what the channels are, and I found that incredibly frightening, and I think that's why I've gone back into the world that I knew before, because I knew those channels.

She would still like to find work in the arts, particularly on projects focusing on cultural diversity, but admits that the transition is very difficult and the competition intense. With hindsight, Amelia now believes that it may have been sensible to spend some of her spare time at the theatre in order to make contacts, network and integrate more fully. With no strong contacts to help her, her jobsearch is focused mainly on newspaper advertisements, which inevitably generate a formidable number of applications. As an interim measure, Amelia has also attempted to secure volunteer work in relevant organisations, but has found that even when she has time to offer free of charge, she is one of many applicants for very few positions. As she has been unable to secure a job appropriate to her career aspirations to date, Amelia is contemplating returning to university for further study.

▶ Joe

Joe taught English as a foreign language in both the UK and Spain before applying to university as a mature student at the age of twenty-five. He is currently in the final year of a degree in Communication, and was required to undertake a six-week work placement at the end of his second year as part of this course. Having had his CV checked by the work placement tutor and having attended relevant workshops, Joe applied for various opportunities and successfully secured a placement at an advertising agency which specialised in both offline advertising campaigns (on billboards and buses) and online campaigns (on specifically targeted websites). This was in keeping with his long-term ambition to 'get into consultancy' and 'look at organisational behaviour and organisational culture'. He recalls that 'I was desperate to get a placement really. And it was media based and I thought it was quite interesting.'

Joe originally applied by email and as a result was invited to attend an interview. The company concerned was in London – 100 miles away from his university and also his home. His travelling expenses were not reimbursed, but Joe thought that it was nevertheless an opportunity worth pursuing:

> I thought it was worth going up. You are driven in that sense. You do sacrifice a bit – you do have to pay for it. There's a bit of peer pressure you know. Everyone is going to London. You feel you have to go. It's a very Londoncentric ideology that is going on there. It's hard. It's hard if you have got to find the cash. You have got to live there for six weeks. All unpaid.

However, Joe was 'very excited. It looked like a very trendy and dynamic organisation. I expected to work reasonably hard and I expected a little of being taken advantage of, as it were. I did expect that to be honest. I was hoping that I would get better admin skills for a start – using Excel and all the office packages. And I expected to learn a lot more about advertising.' But it soon became apparent that the organisation wanted a great deal from Joe. At the interview it was made clear to him that his services were required for nine weeks and not six, which he found worrying in view of the additional financial pressures involved:

> Obviously I didn't want to say 'no' right away, but I felt even if I really enjoyed it I wouldn't be able to stay – not for nine weeks. ... I was fortunate enough to stay with my cousin who lived in zone two, but otherwise I couldn't have done it without a family link. Because you were looking at £85 to £90 for halls of residence which were all booked up anyway for conferences. I accepted on the basis that I would definitely do six weeks. I asked if they were willing to pay after the six weeks and they said 'no'. I said that might be a problem for me. I was fairly clear but I didn't say a definite 'no' at that stage but I said that I might find it difficult to stay.

Joe arrived on his first day to discover that the person who had interviewed him was away on holiday and the full-time employee whom he had been recruited to assist had left on the previous Friday. He was greeted by a supervisor asking if he was the new temp to which he replied that he was the placement student 'because it is very different'. He was left with a colleague who was really too busy with her own work to deal with him.

Joe's work focused on a campaign involving a bank. An advertising campaign had been launched on the Internet, and adverts had been placed on different sites. Joe's job was to research how the campaign had gone from March to June which involved investigating 'the click ratio' – how many hits there had been on each site, compiling the information, evaluating it and writing a short overview. This represented a considerable undertaking, and from the outset there were problems.

> I didn't have any media planning experience and they did know that. I explained it at the interview. And they did say it was Internet based work. I said 'I'm quite

happy with internet based work because you do a lot of it at university with research and so on.' But the saddest thing about it is the guy who interviewed me, the leader, was on holiday. I didn't realise the implications that that would hold. And the girl who was in charge of me – it was not really her responsibility unfortunately. Obviously – why should she look after me? She was not being paid for it. I just needed one day's orientation or two day's orientation to really get into the swing of things, because without that you do feel a little bit pressured because you want to ask for help but there is a culture of fear there where you don't feel you can because they are so busy and stressed.

On the first day Joe had arrived at nine o'clock. At seven o'clock in the evening he was still there. 'I expressed a desire to go home and I was told that I should stay by the person supervising me who had been left in charge of me. So it was that sort of situation. It was a bit unfortunate. I was really disappointed actually.' Joe felt that the company was primarily interested in getting the work out of him with little regard for what constituted reasonable working conditions. He noted that in these circumstances it was essential to be assertive. The situation went from bad to worse as he had not been given sufficient orientation or support:

It got to the stage where on the Thursday I was not producing the work, and I said: 'I can't possibly put a forty-eight page PowerPoint presentation together without a clear understanding of the campaign.' So what you can interpret from this is that they gave me too much responsibility because they were under pressure; they had lost a person, and unfortunately I was in the middle of that situation. End of week one I expressed my desire to move departments and I was told that I couldn't, so I decided to leave straight away. I was a bit worried, and I was feeling really upset about the situation and a bit worried for personal reasons. I was a bit less confident than I usually am and I was a bit exhausted after all my exams. When I got back home I sent an email to my tutor and she explained that I hadn't followed the procedures which were in place and then I was reprimanded by the university for not following the procedures. I found that hard because I know I didn't follow the procedures but I wasn't thinking straight at the time. I sent an email to the company apologising. I didn't get a response to that. They just ignored me. They must have been a bit annoyed but then I really had to make a quick decision because it was expensive. I had tried to address it on the Thursday evening saying I can't prepare this PowerPoint presentation without some help. I can't tell you how a campaign is going from 3 months ago when I've just turned up. There was like – let me get back to you; and then it was me sending emails, and the classic quote was 'Joe don't send me an email if the work is not complete.' I feel that I made the right decision to leave. I'm very outgoing. I'm happy to work. But on a placement you need to feel, at least in the first week, that you are appreciated to a certain extent, that what you are doing is productive, and if it's going wrong, that someone has to give you a little bit of a helping hand. If you were paid to do the job you would be expected to do it properly and they would have to give you some kind of guidance. There was no guidance.

Joe returned to university and immediately set about securing another placement so that he would be allowed to continue with the module. This time he looked in the immediate vicinity to the university, as this would enable him to live more cheaply. Drawing on his previous experience he found a placement at an EFL school and worked on their marketing. He feels that he made a valuable contribution to the organisation, and this was clearly reciprocated as they paid him a salary for his time with them. This time the placement went according to plan, fulfilling his expectations and simultaneously benefiting the host organisation.

▶ Priya

Priya is a twenty-year-old undergraduate currently in the third year of a psychology degree. Her course involves a 'thin sandwich' in which she is expected to undertake six-month work placements in both her second and third years. She has completed one placement and will begin the second shortly. Through her dealings with the university work placement office, Priya opted to work with a family who had an autistic boy, partly because of her long-term ambition to work with children. The job she accepted, which was paid at the rate of £5 per hour, involved working as an applied behavioural analyst in a one-to-one situation with an autistic child. Priya was one of a team of therapists, working three sessions a week for three hours at a time. She and the other therapists who covered different shifts worked to the same programme and were guided and taught by a supervisor from a charity organisation specialising in this type of work who visited every two weeks.

The boy in question was a five-year-old with behavioural difficulties who had a tendency to cry for long periods of time and to become aggressive. Whilst Priya was enthusiastic about her duties and the programme designed to help the child, she experienced problems from the outset:

> Sometimes she [the child's mother] would leave the therapist with her son on her own or sometimes her mum would come. Now it's really hard to do therapy if someone keeps interrupting you. It should be non-interruptive, and if someone says: 'What are you doing?' especially if it's not someone directly involved in the

programme, [it is counter-productive]. So instead of therapy helping the son it became more of a babysitting job. We were thrown into this programme in the deep end and obviously the supervisor only came in once every two weeks. I used to work on my own but there were another three therapists that used to work alongside. They did different days. We all got to know each other because of the programme. A lot of the other tutors felt the same way. I know they did.

The logistics of the arrangement did not run smoothly either:

There was a lot of pressure from the parent because they have a lot of emotional problems themselves and that got inflicted on us. She became very dependent and she didn't want us to leave. Say you needed a day off – it would become a really big ordeal. I was travelling about 2 hours to get there by 2 buses and if I was even 5 minutes late she would go: 'Why are you late?' And I'd even say I'd make it up at the end but it was still not good enough.

Moreover, Priya soon realised that she was not receiving her pay, which, since she was also covering her own travelling expenses meant that she was becoming increasingly out of pocket:

I was only there for about 2 or 3 months and I hadn't been paid at all. She didn't pay me for the first month and she told me that she was waiting for the LEA to pay her so I gave her another couple of weeks and I still wasn't getting paid. So I left it another month and I still wasn't getting paid. Then it ran into the third month and at that time I decided that this was causing a lot of stress. I told her that I wanted to leave and she said that if I left then I wouldn't get paid. And it sort of became a bit of a threat. But I got paid in the end because the uni wrote letters to her.

The final straw came when the mother returned one day to find her son crying, as he was often accustomed to do. She asked Priya: 'Have you done anything to him?', and Priya was very shocked at the implication that she had harmed the child in any way. She felt very uncomfortable that his mother did not seem to trust her and also realised that any accusations of this nature could jeopardise her long-term aim to work with children. At this point, Priya followed her own mother's advice and sought help from her university work placement tutor:

So I went to the work placement office and I was really upset and I said: 'I don't think I can carry this on. I am not getting support from the parent. I'm trying my best to work there.' I didn't really think the fault lay with me. At first I thought: Am I not working hard enough? And I used to work and work and work. And even the supervisor said: 'You are really good' and even the mum thought I was good at some points but obviously the mum is stressed. She has got a lot of problems of her own. Every time I went there there was this atmosphere and I just didn't feel happy at all. And I'm not usually like that. Usually I am happy. I want to go to work. So they [work placement tutors] said: 'Right, fair enough, leave. What do you want to do now? Because obviously you have to fill in your hours.' And I said: 'I still want to do the same job.' And I think they were a little bit shocked. I really believed in the programme and I thought this really could help somebody and I really wanted to work with children. I didn't want to leave and think that I wasn't good enough. Whatever happened I didn't want to be put off it for ever. So I thought OK let me try it with another family then we will see. Was it me? I needed to know.

Priya then went to work with another family with a six-year-old autistic son and from the outset everything was different. Priya was very honest about what had happened in her previous placement, but this time her relationship with the mother of her charge was very good. Moreover she could see that she was making a difference:

I saw the son improving and we saw that we were helping him. It was just really good. It was fulfilling. Every time I'd leave the house, if I came back the next day his mum would say: 'Oh, he said this and he said that' and I thought, I've done that in my session so he's definitely gaining from it. The child was mute when I met him at the beginning. By this time now, we'd got him labelling over fifty objects say like a chair, television – fifty objects. Everything is broken down into really small steps. At first we have to prompt everything so we might have a cup on the table and we'll say: 'Give me the cup' and then we'll prompt him [by taking his arm to the cup] to give it to us. Then we'd do it again and we'd do it again. It would be really intensive. And then we'd fade the prompt after a time. We'd put the cup on the table and say: 'Give me the cup' and hopefully he would give it. And then next time we'd introduce another item on the table with the cup and then we'd randomly rotate the two items after he'd got the second item. So he now knows a lot of labels. On top of that, he is starting to request the things whereas before it was a matter of guessing what he wanted. I really love it. I'm really happy, really happy that the boy has come a long way. And I've been there for now nearly a year and a half. I really want to stay there but I've decided that I want to go on even further and go and work in an ABA[7] school. There are only about three in the country. I've got another work placement for six months so what I was thinking is that I'll do voluntary work there and carry on with the family as well.

---

[7] Applied Behavioural Analysis.

With hindsight, Priya believes that the first placement did benefit her overall development in that it taught her a great deal about the programme and also gave her some experience of dealing with an employer. Moreover, her confidence has grown as a result of her second placement and she has achieved more self-awareness about how she likes to work and what she hopes to gain from it. She is now seriously considering a career working with autistic children and believes that her placements will help when it comes to applying for work. Above all, she is confident that she made the correct decision in seeking a placement in a similar area after her disappointing experience, as this enabled her to prove to herself that the fundamental problems were not down to her, and that in any case she had the strength to overcome them:

> I don't think people should give up just because they have had one bad experi-
> ence. And you do get positive things out of bad experiences as well. If you really
> want to prove [something] to yourself don't give up just because you've had one
> bad experience. I'd really like to say that to people. Because a lot of people just
> give up don't they. And that might be their dream but it can be shattered. But you
> just have to keep picking yourself up I think.

▶ Jessica

Jessica is 16 years old and is planning a career in hotel management. Having sat for her GCSEs at the end of year eleven, she undertook a two-week work placement at a hotel near her home. Although Jessica's school had the facilities to find placements for their students, she preferred to make her own arrangements, assuming that this would increase the likelihood of finding relevant work that closely matched her aspirations. Having located a hotel that was willing to offer a work placement, Jessica went in for an initial meeting:

> We talked over what I was going to do and how I was going to spend my
> two weeks. She was really nice and we went over everything I was going to do.
> I was going to do meetings and events; work in the restaurant and in reception;
> work in the office doing sales; ringing people up and organising wedding recep-
> tions. She basically said: 'We shall spread your time with everything, and
> then you can have a bit of everything.' I expected a big variety in what I was
> going to do, and I thought it would be fun and experience of the world of work
> and how it was going to be. I thought it might make me want to work in the hotel
> business more.

Jessica had been asked to wear a white shirt and black trousers or a skirt, and on arrival she was given a waistcoat and directed to the restaurant.

> So I went to the restaurant and I helped with breakfast, and I think I spent the whole day in the restaurant until about five [o'clock] I think it was – waitressing. And they made me hoover on my first day! I felt that I did not want to go in the next day basically because they said: 'Tomorrow you will be doing the same.'

Jessica decided not to say anything, because although it was made clear to her that she would be working in the restaurant on her second day, she was promised a change after that. She was reluctant to complain at that stage as she had only been on work placement for a day. At the time it did not occur to her to ask her tutor for help because she took the view that the placement was of a limited duration and she felt she could cope with the timescale involved: 'I thought it's only for two weeks. I can survive it. And it's just taught me a lesson of what I don't really want to do.' She spent most of her time in the first week waitressing and cleaning:

> I cleaned a piano in the restaurant and hoovered between breakfast and lunch. I spent ages cleaning plates and polishing cutlery, because when the restaurant is open there's breakfast, lunch and dinner and there is a massive gap between them so you have to clean all the plates and polish all the cutlery. The other girl that was doing work experience was doing it as well. ... They made me do the tasks that just anyone could do. Working in the restaurant didn't really teach me anything because I could already do it. ... I think it's just that they were busy. I think if I went in the quiet season they would have more that I could do because they would have time to train me.

Fortunately for Jessica, the second week was better than the first in that it was more varied. On the second Monday she was stationed in reception. However, since all the bookings were on a computer system she was not invited to help with the actual work, but instead watched others dealing with routine tasks and the day-to-day running of reception. Although Jessica believes that she would have been able to master the computer system by the end of the day had the basics been outlined to her, the relevant staff were too busy to teach her. Later in the second week she was scheduled to help with 'meetings and events operations' but, when the time came for her to start, the supervisor in charge of the section confessed that he did not have time to train her and indicated that he was reluctant to have her attached to his section. As a result, Jessica went back to the person who had organised her work placement and helped her for the day.

This turned out to be a more interesting alternative, as it meant that Jessica was able to gain an insight into the working of the personnel office. 'I enjoyed shadowing. It showed me what other people's jobs were and whether I'd like to do them, and what they have to do.' Some new employees were due to arrive from South Africa and Jessica helped to organise their rooms and involved herself in the administrative preparations for their arrival.

Another positive aspect of the placement was the experience of workplace culture and the interaction with colleagues.

> The people there were really, really nice. I really liked them. And at the end of my two weeks I was upset to leave them. Most of them were quite young. They were doing their summer work from uni. Everyone was friendly to each other and everyone got on. They did work as part of a team. When I was in the restaurant I definitely felt part of it. And then when you get into the office the people are quite a bit older. That was fine because they treat you like you are working. They don't treat you like a student on work experience. They talk to you like an adult as if you are working.

With the benefit of hindsight, Jessica feels that she could have handled the situation differently, particularly as the hotel staff invited feedback and she was given several opportunities to express her opinions:

> They kept asking me if I was enjoying myself and I didn't want to say 'no', so I said: 'Yes, I'm having a really good time.' I should have said I wanted to have more variety and it was just getting a bit repetitive doing waitressing. I just didn't want to tell them I wasn't enjoying it because they had spent time organising it. I would have had a much better 2 weeks if I had done something about not enjoying it. But I didn't want to make a fuss. I wish I had and then I might have got more experience, but it just taught me for next time, if I do work experience again.

Jessica would also have asked for a 'specific plan' for each day and would have ensured that it was adhered to by both parties. She felt that she didn't learn very much from waitressing, particularly as this was the sort of work that she could have done elsewhere with the advantage of being paid for her services, whereas on this occasion she was unpaid. Jessica is under the impression that after she and the other work placement student left, the hotel hired waitresses to fill their shoes and paid the people concerned. This has led to her view that the hotel's primary objective was to use her to cover its own needs 'because they were busy and they needed the help in the restaurant' rather than to consider her own needs as a work placement student. She now reflects that: 'I think they knew what they were going to use me for but I was really naïve and I thought I'm going to have a really great time and I'm going to experience everything.'

After the placement came to an end the hotel filled in an assessment form about Jessica which invited comments about her appearance, attitude and so on. The results were complimentary, which for Jessica went some way towards redeeming the situation. However, she nevertheless admits that 'I was relieved it was over.'

10 Written and Oral Assignments

This chapter will suggest guidelines for:

- ▶ keeping a learning log/diary
- ▶ writing a reflective essay
- ▶ giving a presentation
- ▶ writing a report

It is very likely that in addition to attending your work placement you will be expected to undertake certain assignments in order to gain full credit for your endeavours. Moreover, even if no assignments are set, students may like to consider tackling one or two on a voluntary basis, since this will help personal development by clarifying and organising thoughts and observations and illuminating the learning outcomes. As the requirements tend to vary from one institution to another, it is very important to be clear about what is expected from you. The following guidelines offer suggestions as to how to keep a learning log or diary, write a reflective essay and report and give a presentation, as these are assignments that are commonly associated with work placement modules in many universities. However, it is of course essential that students ensure that the work they submit conforms precisely to what is required by their particular institution. The methodology suggested here may need to be amended in order to ensure that the assignment fulfils all the criteria and requirements of the university.

In terms of most assignments, students will get better grades if they are able to relate their observations and learning on work experience to the theoretical ideas that they have covered in their university course work. If students are able to demonstrate an understanding of how theory and practice relate and interact at this stage, it is more likely that in their future careers they will be able to use theoretical knowledge to improve practical procedures in the workplace.

▶ Keeping a learning log/work placement diary

The key to submitting a high quality learning log relies in the first place on having sufficient data and in the second place on drawing relevant and astute observations from it. Since it is not always obvious what constitutes 'good' data, the best strategy is to keep a note of everything as you go along on the basis that you can always select what, with hindsight, has the most useful content and at that point you can write out a new log if necessary. Once you accept that the log you carry around with you will not be the one you hand in, it frees you from having to make difficult decisions about what to include at the time. It also means that neatness is not an issue. This is important as you may not always have time to present your notes to their best visual advantage, or even legibly! You should focus on content at this stage and worry about presentation only when you are working on the final version.

It is very important that you take your log/diary everywhere with you whilst you are at work. It is better to jot down notes on the events of the day at the time and then add more details later, although if this is not possible you should set aside some time at the end of each day to write your log whilst your thoughts are still fresh in your mind. It is essential that the log is 'for your eyes only' and that you take measures to keep its contents private. If you are concerned that your notes will be read, this will discourage you from being totally honest. If you do not want to take the risk of others seeing your log, write your reflective comments at home on paper as these can be inserted later, and restrict the entries made at work to a breakdown of the structure of your day.

A good place to start is with a timetable, including your arrival time; scheduled meetings; time spent on specific tasks; shadowing; visits to different departments; breaks and so on. At the time, write down enough information to refresh your memory later when you come to add supplementary details. Later, when you are comfortable with the log/diary format, you can be selective, and only note down events that showed you something new about yourself, or reinforced previous thoughts, or tested a particular skill. You should include significant comments made about your work, whether congratulatory or critical and note events and occurrences that you consider to represent an achievement or a marker of progress on your part. After each entry, leave a reasonable gap so that you can log your observations later, and leave a large gap at the end of each day's timetable so that you can insert an overview for the day in question if appropriate. The basic information to note might include the following elements.

Meetings

You should note the starting and finishing times of the meeting; who was present; the purpose of the meeting and who called it. During the meeting you might like to note: important points that were made; and by whom; the reaction these comments caused; changes in the direction of the meeting and the response of participants; any particularly successful or unsuccessful strategies on the part of the speakers; your own contribution if you made one, and the overall atmosphere and outcome. Later, when you have had time to deliberate, you should add your own assessment as to whether or not the meeting achieved its purpose and why; whether you learnt anything from the experience; whether anything surprised you; and whether with hindsight you could see a better way of achieving the outcome.

Tasks

Log the tasks you do and how long you spend on them. Later, you might add a brief description of the task; any problems you encountered; the skills that were called upon; whether you felt you coped adequately, inadequately or well; whether others helped you and if so how clearly you were taught and how easily you learnt; and what you took away from the experience. If you are likely to be engaged in a similar task over a long period of time you might like to time yourself to estimate whether or not your speed is improving. Do not limit yourself to practical work tasks. It is very important that you also track how well you are integrating into the workplace; how easy or difficult you find it to communicate and interact with your colleagues, and how successfully you are able to explain your views and opinions. You should note down how *you* feel you coped with each situation you write about, plus any supporting evidence of progress, such as other people's comments. Try not to write purely descriptive accounts, but instead, focus on the underlying rationale and try to see how the situation could have been avoided, or could be improved next time.

Shadowing

If you are shadowing someone else you should note how their day is spent and what you observed them doing. Later, you might add what you learnt from their performance and whether you were impressed or unimpressed by specific aspects of it. Think about whether you would like to undertake similar work and whether or not you would be good at it, and try to account for your reasons. This may help you to pinpoint your own potential areas for improvement.

Visits
Note any visits to other departments or organisations plus any field trips. Later you might compare these to the running and atmosphere of your own workplace. Were the visits useful in contributing to an overall picture of the product or industry? What did you learn? Did this surprise you?

Lunch breaks
Note how you spend your lunch breaks. Are you alone or with others, on site or outside the workplace? This may seem unimportant, but it is actually a way of measuring how well you are accepted by your colleagues. Over time you may notice that you are included socially on a more regular basis. If you take your break with others, write down how comfortable you are with the situation and your reasons.

Overall view
At the end of a few days, you might re-read several entries and see if you can discern progress of any kind, whether in terms of increased social integration in the workplace; other's attitudes towards your work contribution or your own perception of your skills or your output. Hopefully, you will progressively become more honest in critiquing your work, and more likely to be able to identify the focal point of problems and issues. When your work placement has finished, it would be a good idea to re-read the entire log and jot down your immediate thoughts as some of these observations will form the basis for your reflective essay.

▶ Writing a reflective essay

Although there are several areas of overlap between a learning log and a reflective essay, there are also fundamental differences. Clearly, the format for each varies considerably, with a reflective essay employing continuous prose and a learning log tending to be organised under a series of headings and sub-headings, arranged around a basic timetable. Moreover, there are also differences as to the scope, emphasis and perspective involved. A reflective essay is first and foremost an account of your personal observations about your workplace environment, and most particularly your own acclimatisation and development within it, and your consequent analysis of what this means in terms of your future career strategy and development. You may find the following sub-headings helpful in planning your reflective essay. They do not represent an exhaustive list, but are guidelines about the information you might wish to include.

What attracted you to this placement/ sector of industry?

Whilst a learning log starts when you arrive at your work placement on the first day, the reflective essay can begin long before that. You might like to start with the rationale underpinning your choice of placement. You may wish to present some background information at this point to put what follows into context. Remember that an External Examiner, who does not know you, may read your reflective essay, so it is worth allocating a few paragraphs to setting the scene. This background information is also useful in indicating your own assessment of your skills, personal attributes and career aspirations at that time which directed you towards a particular line of work or sector. However, whilst a short introduction is helpful, do not be tempted to dwell on this section. It should remain concise and brief as the major proportion of the essay should focus on your critical evaluation of your performance within the context of the placement.

What were your preconceived ideas? Were they accurate?

Hopefully, your knowledge of the organisation or profession in question, together with your appraisal of the daily work involved, developed and broadened during the course of your placement. A good way of illustrating this is to note down early on in your reflective essay any preconceived ideas you may have had prior to starting your placement. Later you can expand on this, describing how these ideas and opinions may have changed over time and identifying what provoked the change.

What have you learnt about the sector in which you have been working?

The purpose of this question is not to elicit statistical data, but to give you the opportunity to show a broad awareness both of this environment and also your own development in the context of this particular setting. It may include comments on the operating processes of the organisation, for example, how the staff hierarchy functions; whether people tend to work in teams or on individual projects; whether communication between people is generally verbal or written; whether staff are called upon to make decisions quickly or whether there is time to deliberate, and on the overall atmosphere of the organisation. A clear analysis of this will help you to identify the skills and personal attributes that are key to surviving and thriving in this sector. You can then relate these findings to yourself in particular.

What were the learning outcomes from the placement?

Identifying what you learnt from the placement is likely to be a major component of your reflective essay. You have probably learnt a great deal in many different senses, so it is important to arrange your thoughts into a logical order. Broadly, you are likely to have encountered new experiences; practised new skills and developed the ones you already possessed; formed some view of workplace culture and the unwritten 'rules' of the workplace; interacted with other members of staff on both work and social levels and dealt with the practical details of working life, such as dressing and behaving appropriately and arriving on time. Whenever you identify a learning outcome, try to give an example in order to substantiate your opinion. Focus particularly on whether or not the placement has been helpful in the sense of advancing your own personal development and skills and try to account for the thought processes underpinning your views. It is perfectly acceptable to be anecdotal, provided that you use the example to support a broader claim or observation. If possible, try to evaluate your own progress and development, perhaps by noting if it was reflected in the comments and attitudes of others towards you. Do not forget to discuss how you actually *felt* both during and after the placement, and try to look beyond these immediate feelings to their implications, for example, whether they might mean that you are now more confident about certain career aspirations.

Has the placement helped you make career decisions?

You may find that in the course of undertaking the placement you began to develop firmer ideas about what you would like to do in terms of your future career. Both positive and negative thoughts can be helpful in this respect. It is just as useful to discover how you do not want to spend your time as to find out what you enjoy most from the workplace environment. In dealing with this question, you might find it helpful first of all to note down which tasks you particularly liked or did not like, before looking beyond the actual task to what it involved that prompted your specific reaction. You may discover, for example, that you found repetitive tasks unfulfilling or that you particularly liked building on ideas suggested by others or witnessing others develop your initial suggestions. What do these observations say about you as a potential member of staff? What are the implications in terms of future career decisions?

Your completed reflective essay should show that you have thought critically about each significant aspect of the work placement and set these findings within the context of your own personal attributes, skills and preferences. Ideally, you should be able to draw conclusions from this exercise that will help you in making future career decisions.

▶ Giving a presentation

If you are required to give a presentation on your work placement it is essential to think through the structure and form this might take whilst you are actually undertaking the placement, as this will enable you to gather any appropriate supporting materials and check relevant details at the time. If you leave this until you have left it will be far more difficult and time consuming.

Timescale
The fundamental rule if you are asked to give a presentation is to plan your work well so that it fits neatly into the allocated time slot whilst simultaneously delivering an appropriate amount of information to the audience. If you have too much information, your presentation will appear rushed and the audience will not be able to absorb all the details, and if you have too little information, the presentation will appear to flag and your audience may become bored. Check whether or not there will be time for questions, and if so, how much time. Practice reading a page of prose slowly as this will give you a guide as to how many words you might expect to deliver in the course of your presentation. However, remember that with pauses and ad lib comments, your written notes should ideally underrun slightly.

The audience
Your audience is likely to comprise members of staff from your department, your peers and possibly an examiner from elsewhere. The implication of this is that none of the aforementioned is likely to be an expert in the workings of your placement organisation and fortunately, they are likely to be very sympathetic. As you are speaking to an intelligent audience that is largely uninformed about the subject of your presentation, this means that it is important that you pick out the key points and do not delve too heavily into minutiae. By comparison, if you were speaking to a group from your workplace, you could assume that they knew the key facts and that the interest for them would specifically lie in your observations about the finer points.

Structure and content
Think carefully about what the assignment calls for and adjust your material accordingly. If the presentation is designed to give the audience an overview of your placement, think in terms of sections of information.

The opening sentences are very important and should attract the attention of your audience. Very early on you should give some indication of the structure of your presentation, and a visual aid could help here. Whilst preparing what you wish to say, break your presentation down into bullet points, with major headings and subordinate headings, and arrange your material around this structure. You may wish to start with a brief overview of the sector before moving on to your particular organisation, and then to your role whilst on placement. In terms of the organisation you may wish to include facts and figures about the product; the main objectives of the organisation; location; numbers of employees; funding and so on. In the case of a large company, you might display an organisation chart to indicate where your contribution came in. If your overall presentation, including questions, should be approximately twenty minutes in length, then imagine that you have five minutes to explain to someone about the sector, then another five to explain the workings of the company and then another five to talk about your own position. This is effectively what you will be doing in your presentation. Start with the wider picture and then focus in on details later as by then your audience will be able to put your comments into context. You cannot cover everything, so do not try to. Instead, select the key points and focus on them. In a presentation of this length, your audience cannot be expected to absorb hundreds of facts. However, they will appreciate hearing perhaps half a dozen new ideas, supported by interesting details. Your conclusion is vital. It should draw your presentation together with a few well-chosen sentences summarising what you have said and leaving your audience with a clear impression of the overall sense of your presentation. If there are no questions at all, be prepared to speak for a further three minutes, perhaps on how you now feel about your academic studies having returned to university, or perhaps by offering your overview of placements in general. Once again, rehearse a strong and clear final sentence.

Visuals
Visuals such as slides, PowerPoint effects and even artefacts themselves can bring a presentation to life for the audience. If you are using overheads or an equivalent, a good rule of thumb is to show one for every three to four minutes of speaking, if appropriate. Slides are particularly useful. You can illustrate statistics visually for example in graphs; you can show pictures of buildings, machinery, stills from theatrical productions and so on. It is a good idea to avoid slides containing paragraphs of words because, if they are not identical to your spoken words, you are asking your audience to imbibe and digest two messages simultaneously, which is problematic, and if they do reflect your speech exactly they are arguably unnecessary.

However, committing your main headings to overheads can be useful and can keep your presentation on track. If you do this, ensure that you show the appropriate overhead that will synchronise with your speech. You can use visuals to lighten up a series of facts or to illustrate statistics that might otherwise be difficult to visualise. Ensure that all visuals are legible and keep images as simple as possible for maximum effect.

It is important to check what facilities will be available in the room in which you will give your presentation. You may have to fill in a form in advance to request an overhead projector or PowerPoint facilities. If your presentation is on PowerPoint, ensure that you also bring a set of overheads as, if there are any problems with the computer technology, there may not be time to restart and you may have to continue without your PowerPoint graphics. If you are using an overhead projector, check that you know how to turn the machine on and which way up to put on your acetates, and if you are not sure, arrive early and try it out. Keep your visuals in the order in which you wish to display them and practise peeling off their covers. Decide beforehand where you will put acetates after you have used them so that you do not mix them up with those remaining.

You may wish to hand round artefacts that complement your presentation or indeed to provide a handout of further details.

Delivery
Delivering a presentation well is mostly a matter of practice, although there are some basic rules. Preparation is the key to success. Plan your presentation well in advance and rehearse it at least once. Remember that written English and spoken English generally differ in tone and style, and your presentation will benefit from an informal, conversational tone. It is a good idea to write out your presentation even if you intend to learn it, as if you do have a memory lapse your notes will provide an aide memoire. If you insert headings and subheadings into the written version, you may well find that a list of these on a separate card is all you need to remind you of the next stage. Some people find it helpful to speak from a series of cards, the advantage being that these are small and easier to manage than pages of A4 paper. Whatever you choose, try not to read verbatim from your notes. If you extemporise, you are more likely to build a rapport with your audience. Be careful not to stand in front of the overhead projector screen and try to look up at your audience as much as possible. Establishing eye contact will enhance rapport, but you should avoid looking at one person in particular. Don't wear jewellery that jangles, and remember that if you wish to make use of a radio microphone it is useful to be wearing something with a pocket suitable to house the battery. Take a deep breath before you start and try not to race. Speak slowly and clearly, and avoid the use of

jargon. Try to ensure that your voice is audible at all times. Make sure that there are breaks, for example, when you change your overhead transparencies, as they will be a welcome breathing space for both you and your audience. Don't be afraid of silences, but use them to your advantage, for example, after you have made a major point and wish to give your audience time to digest what you have said.

Dealing with questions

Try not to anticipate problems. The questions are likely to be based on your presentation, which, of course, you wrote yourself and know well. Take your time in answering and if you do not understand the question ask for clarification, or more details. If you are asked a very complicated question and you do not have time to answer it fully, state this and then talk about the single most important aspect of it. If you do not know the answer, you should say so, but if it is an interesting area that you would like to explore later, you can state that too. When you have finished answering questions, make it clear that the presentation is now over, by, for example, thanking your audience. Do not spoil the effect by displaying obvious relief. Maintain your professionalism as you collect your visuals and return to your seat.

▶ Writing a report

Style and tone

Writing a report differs from the other assignments covered in this chapter in two main ways. First, it does not call for subjective or self-reflective comments, and indeed, an objective stance is optimum. The focus here is on the actual organisation, not on your impressions of it or any effect on you personally arising from the research. Secondly, it requires a much wider perspective as it is only really possible to report on one organisation if the writer is aware of comparisons within the sector as a whole. You are likely to have to do more research for this piece of work than for some of the other assignments and you are likely to be dealing with more statistical and factual data. Reports tend to be written in the third person and the overall tone is likely to be comparatively formal and impersonal.

Content

Your report might start by locating the organisation concerned within its market sector by describing the purpose of the business and the part it plays within the sector as a whole. Details should include the relative size of the business in terms of turnover, staffing levels and accommodation, and its positioning in terms of importance and function within the sector.

You should also mention whether it is a producer or whether it outsources its production. If you are working in the voluntary sector, you could list the key objectives of your organisation and how these are achieved in terms of manpower and resources. The financial health of the company or organisation is very important so your report should include a financial analysis, detailing how revenue is raised and how it is spent. If your organisation is a commercial one, you might include an appraisal of its positioning in relation to its competitors. You could analyse how the business is organised and comment on the hierarchy. Finally, you might look to future expectations and aspirations, although, since this cannot be based on undisputed facts, it is important to indicate the reasons underlying your assessment, plus your sources.

Sources for information

Once again, researching and collecting data for your report will be far easier if undertaken whilst you are actually on your placement. Most companies have an employee specifically responsible for public relations, if not an actual department devoted to this work. This is a valuable resource for any press releases, newspaper articles about the company and indeed public relations literature, for example about new products, and significant changes of direction for the company. If it is a large organisation, the report and accounts are likely to contain useful information, both on the financial affairs of the business and also on the milestones from the previous year that are deemed by the board to be of the greatest significance. You may also wish to take your own photographs. If there are any gaps in your information, send an email to the relevant person for an answer to your questions, or ask if he or she will give you a short interview if convenient. In the event of the latter you should prepare your questions beforehand and tape the interview. In either case you can use the relevant quotations to cover important areas for which there is little or no supporting literature. In all cases it is a good idea to cross check your information for accuracy with at least one other source, and to reference your sources of information so that it is clear whether or not you are relying on facts or a personal opinion.

► Summary

This chapter has offered guidelines on keeping a learning log; writing a reflective essay; giving a presentation and writing a report. Although there are areas of overlap in these assignments, the perspective and emphasis of each is unique. Broadly speaking, the learning log charts what you did and what you learnt; the reflective essay evaluates your observations and development in the course of achieving the learning outcomes; the presentation offers a brief overview of the organisation, identifies the specific contribution made by your department and focuses on your own work in particular; and the report looks at the organisation from a more objective viewpoint, noting its size, output, finances, operating procedures and policies and situating these observations in the wider context of the sector as a whole.

Perspectives and Feedback

Our students' placements are assessed by a portfolio which should include an analysis of the host organisation and an assessment of their own self-development. Students commonly lose marks in the portfolio in the following two ways: firstly they are overly descriptive about the work experience itself, sometimes providing a day-by-day account of tea-making and envelope stuffing rather than an insightful evaluation of their learning! Secondly they often seem to forget all about the taught courses that preceded their placement and don't refer to theories, models and concepts covered in courses or indeed reference their work with academic texts. It's understandable to a certain extent that the world of academia is forgotten whilst students are in the working world but in order to gain good marks students need to demonstrate that they understand the integration of these two worlds.

Naomi, *tutor*

I had to write a 5,000-word report after my placement which was assessed by the university. I found it a worthwhile exercise to consolidate all that I had learnt. Partly because it will be helpful when people i.e. future employees ask me what my responsibilities were and what skills I learnt from the experience, but also because it gave me a sense of the achievements I had made.

Fiona, *student*

Students often ask me about the value of learning logs. I think that their main contribution is to improve students' skills of analysis and problem solving and to help them develop skills of critical reflection. If students are to complete in a global market place and be on the 'cutting edge' then knowledge of how to learn is as important as the content of what they learn. In preparing students to use learning logs, journals or reflective diaries it is essential to introduce them to the process in a systematic way and give clear examples of what is expected. Many logs are often too descriptive and students fail to move beyond this to reflect on the events they are describing. Reflection is not a simple concept and students need help and coaching in what we mean by being reflective. I have often offered students a fairly prescriptive structure in the first instance but allowed flexibility for individuals that wish to record their learning experiences in other formats. Students who achieve high marks in their logs are able to strike a good balance between description, reflection and action planning. A succinct description of the context is what is required followed by reflection on this. Students also often fail to integrate theoretical or conceptual models into their reflective diaries, therefore often making their reflections too personal and bland.

Colin, *tutor*

I found it a little bit repetitive – ticking off boxes. The main issue was that apart from written feedback there was nothing to be said by the tutors. Before the placement it was stressed how important it was and how insightful the log books were and that it was so important to fill them in, but at the end of the day they were simply handed back to the student, no further comment, no verbal expression of praise – NOTHING! You have appraised yourself and been appraised by your company but at the end of it there is no [verbal] feedback. Students perceived this as a trivial approach to their efforts. It almost seemed like having to look at the log books was a bit of a chore that lecturers could have done without but this is purely speculation as the written feedback was quite thorough. Still, verbal feedback should be equally as important in my and many of my friends' opinion.

Joe, *student*

Students on the work experience modules are required to submit a report as part of their assessment. The report represents almost a third of their final grade and it's designed to demonstrate that they have achieved certain of the learning outcomes specified at the beginning of the module. In reality, it is engineered to help the students take stock of the whole experience and what they have learned. It's less reflective than the logbook that they also submit, but the student must show evidence of a global understanding of their work environment from the industry through to the particular role/function that they fulfilled and also how this experience will impact on their future career. The students are encouraged to be discursive and we give them thorough guidelines on what to include. However, the biggest barrier for students seems to be going beyond the superficial day-to-day commentary and really analysing what is going on around them in the workplace. Once they get into the habit of being analytical at work, then the report is much easier to write. We've even had students who've managed to do that and then complain that the word count (1,500) is too limited to enable them to develop their observations to their contentment!

Liesbeth – *tutor*

The log books have helped me track my thoughts and add data as I go along. They will be useful sources for me, not just for my other assignments but also for my future working life. I can look back to read my comments on the companies I went to.

Judi, *student*

Presentations are too easily dismissed as a by-product of work placement modules whose main role is to provide an accessible form of assessment. In fact, the presentation session is the one occasion when all students share their enthusiasm, their success and their experience with a wider audience. It is often only at the point of preparation for presentations that students are forced to think reflectively about their placements. Presentations require students to explain clearly and accessibly what went right and it provides them with a forum in which to articulate what went wrong and why. In doing so it allows them and their peers to compare experiences and to reflect critically on them. Finally, many of these students learn about effective non-academic modes of communication while on placements and the presentation format gives them the opportunity to deploy these new found skills.

Annie – *tutor*

I had to write a report on what I'd done. I did find it useful in that I did want to read more about xxx and whatever I did read it helped me to understand it more. I used the reading for the report. It was 5,000 words. It was really good. We got to find out about what we were doing from different angles.

Priya, *student*

Education on the course I administer is a 'learning by doing' process, where the acquisition and application of knowledge and skills is manifest in a substantial portfolio of work. It is understandable that whilst students explore work-focused and work-related issues in the context of university knowledge, scholarship and values, students are sometimes unaware that they are acquiring new skills or developing existing ones while at work. Work-based learning – in the context of the personal development plan – will guide students to develop the practice of identifying their learning at work so that the concept of life-long learning is enhanced.

Sam, *tutor*

I think the reflective essay is a little bit self-indulgent. Maybe it justifies the way you feel when there is no need to. I don't think it should be part of a university module.

Amelia, *student*

We have to do a presentation for this work placement module and it was interesting because it made me realise how much I had actually learnt. I was also surprised that I was able to talk so easily in my presentation about the charity to a live audience and answer any questions that they had about it. But just through my two weeks there I had learnt the ropes much more than I thought I had, and had a good enough knowledge about the way the office worked and about their projects.

Katrina, *student*

11 From Work Placement to Employment

This chapter will give key pointers on:

- ▶ what you need to do after your work placement ends
- ▶ how to create a jobsearch strategy
- ▶ a positive outlook for job hunting
- ▶ alternative courses of action

The process of locating, securing and attending a work placement is effectively a micro jobsearch experience. This means that students who have completed a work placement are in a very advantageous position when it comes to seeking employment after graduation. All the relevant skills required to find and undertake work have already been brought to the fore and tested, and hopefully, the student has developed both personally and professionally due not only to the work placement experience itself, but also as a result of the learning outcomes from each stage of the procedure. This chapter will focus on finding employment after graduation, and in so doing it will revisit some of the key observations and findings from earlier chapters.

▶ Post-placement action required

Frequently, work placements are undertaken in the penultimate year of a university course, or in various vacations, which means that there is often still some time before graduation. As it is important not to forget any lessons which may have been learnt or any suggestions for improvement which may have arisen during the course of the placement, it is inadvisable to put your work placement out of your mind as soon as it is finished. Spending an hour or so 'wrapping up' your placement, and taking any action required as a result, will reap dividends later. Therefore, while the experience is still fresh in your memory, take the time to reflect upon your placement and to identify any 'gaps' in your skills that have still not been filled. You can then decide upon a strategy to address any problem areas over the ensuing months. A de-briefing evaluative session with your work placement tutor can be very helpful, and if you do not have a tutor, this is something that can usefully be done by a group of your friends.

Reflecting on your work placement

Writing a self-reflective essay as a module assignment is probably the best way to organise your thoughts about your work placement. Even if this is not mandatory within your university, it is worth considering. If you do not have sufficient time to write an essay, you should at the very least make comprehensive notes to which you may refer later. You are likely to discover that your own writing not only gives expression to your self-awareness but also that it provides practical pointers as to future career decisions. Note what you learnt and list any new skills acquired. Write down anything you particularly enjoyed and felt you could do well, and also indicate what you found less interesting or difficult.

Identifying 'gaps'

With the benefit of hindsight, make a list of all the skills and attributes that the ideal candidate for your work placement should possess. Then try to take a critical step back and identify what you found problematic whilst on work placement and where you felt your own limitations and weaknesses let you down. If you can perceive 'gaps' in your skills and attitude, now is the time to address them. If, for example, you found working as part of a team difficult, then opt for teamwork assignments in your remaining university modules; if you found it difficult to talk about your work to others, offer to give a short presentation when a tutor next looks for a volunteer. There are many opportunities to improve within the actual university environment, but if you prefer to hone your skills elsewhere, you can always offer your services outside, for example by approaching a charity of your choice or by answering an appeal for help. The careers service at your university may also be able to help you with advice relating to a specific problem.

If, as a result of your work placement, you have now revised your ideas completely in terms of what you would like to do after graduation, it may be necessary to prove your commitment to your new choice of career in some way. Undoubtedly some of what you have learnt will still be relevant and useful, but you may find that now you do not have demonstrable experience in the sector in which you are currently interested. If this is the case do not wait until after graduation to remedy the situation, but try to address it before you leave. Whilst it may be unrealistic to try to gain more work experience at this stage, you may still be able to attend a relevant open day, lecture or conference. You can find out about these possibilities from the relevant trade press, the university job shop and by searching the Internet. It is important to do what you can to prove your commitment to add credibility to any job application you may make in the future. Although it is never too late to do this, in today's competitive marketplace employers may well favour candidates who take time and effort to investigate the opportunities available, and clearly it is more convincing if an applicant's interest may be traced back several months rather than if it appears to coincide with the publication of a particular job advertisement.

▶ Jobsearch action plan

As you approach the end of your final year, it is wise to construct a jobsearch action plan. This will ensure that you have collected all the materials and information you require in good time; that you have drafted the blueprint of your basic application; that you have set a system in place whereby you can research relevant organisations and note your findings, and that you have set up a filing system to keep track of all your applications. Once these arrangements are made, you will find tackling each individual job application much easier. Prior to doing this, you may find it useful to re-read Chapters 2 and 3 as this process is similar to that underlying the search for a work placement, but on a larger scale.

Revising data

The first step is to update and revise all the information you have about yourself. Start by making a skills audit based on the list of skills you originally compiled when looking for a work placement. By referring to your learning log, reflect upon what you did and what you learnt whilst on placement and make the necessary additions. You may find it helpful to write down examples of specific tasks that drew on particular skills. Try to express this as succinctly as possible and include any new skills that you have learnt as a result of your university coursework too. Having completed your skills audit, you then need to update your list of personal attributes in the same way. In so doing, it is important that you use the same language as your potential employer as this is the best way of selling yourself. Whilst it is important to avoid unnecessary jargon, you should describe your achievements in a similar language to that found in advertisements as this gives the impression of a good match between supply and demand. If you are unsure as to how to do this, look carefully at the requirements expressed in a variety of advertisements and adapt your own list of attributes accordingly. Make a note of your weaknesses too, as it is important that you are aware of them and that you have an accurate picture of yourself. Finally, using the information on these lists, compose a new CV that reflects your current position in terms of skills, achievements, talents and focus. Print out a copy and glance at it from time to time in case new ideas occur to you. Although you will need to customise your CV and letter of application to suit each individual application, you now have all the basic information about yourself at your fingertips.

Identifying preferences

The second stage it to reflect upon your requirements and preferences, as this will ensure that you do not apply for vacancies that are inappropriate for you. As I noted in Chapter 2, you need to consider areas such as finance; location; your own personal circumstances; whether you have strong preferences for a large or small organisation and whether or not the over-riding philosophy of the company, for example whether it is commercial or not for profit, is important to you. However, unlike the work placement situation, this time you also need to consider the potential prospects that come with the job or company in question. Ask yourself what you hope to achieve in the long-term, and try to look at the job in question objectively and assess whether it is a viable stepping-stone on your chosen career path. It is not always easy to estimate career development, and you may wish to raise the issue of future prospects if you are invited for interview. The main purpose of self-reflection at this stage, however, is to ensure that you do not unknowingly proceed at a tangent but that your actions are in keeping with your future aspirations.

You also need to take a very practical approach to job hunting this time. You may, for example, have commuted a very long distance to your placement, which may have been acceptable in the short term but would not be viable for a permanent job. This time you need to decide whether you are prepared to move to be near your job, or whether you need to find a job within a particular radius of a fixed location. You may have very firm ideas about what you want in terms of work but you may not be offered what you want immediately you leave university. It is very important to consider what to do if these circumstances arise. You will need an income, but you may be reluctant to take on a job that you do not want in case you miss a better opportunity. Realistically, whilst you can change your job at any time, it is not wise to accept anything advertised as a permanent post if you intend to drop it at the earliest opportunity.

There are several options open to you if you find yourself in this position. You may choose to return home where your family and friends may be sympathetic to the situation and where living expenses may therefore be considerably lower, and from this position you may choose to take casual work. The problem with this is that it may take longer than you anticipate to locate and achieve the job offer you want, and whilst casual work is easy to explain in the short term, it may go against you if you have been undertaking unskilled work for a considerable time. If you can only find casual work and you have the stamina for a six-day week, try to liberate a day during the week and use that time to apply for an unpaid job shadowing within a relevant organisation, as you can use this experience to bolster your CV. If you want to hold out for your first choice of permanent work, a possible option might be to try to find temporary positions, perhaps through an agency, in a relevant area, as that way you are improving your prospects whilst waiting. Another option would be to select a second choice, but one that is likely to enable you to achieve your first choice of job in the foreseeable future. This might involve taking a different type of job albeit one that is in the right area or with a relevant organisation, as this will enable you to build up contacts and experience. Some students offer a limited amount of their time free of charge in order to gain more work experience in a relevant area, but obviously this presents financial dilemmas. If you have a particular organisation in mind, ask which agency they use for temporary work and investigate that route. Also, set yourself a time limit after which you will revise your strategy. Although this will hopefully not be necessary, it is important to have reflected upon the possibility.

Looking for opportunities

It is very important to identify where to find out about job opportunities and to check these sources regularly. A good starting point is your university job shop or careers service, which is likely to publish lists of vacancies together with notification of employer presentations scheduled to take place at the university. You can also obtain *Prospects Finalist* and *Prospects Today* magazines from the job shop, or you may choose to purchase these publications direct by subscribing to Graduate Prospects (www.prospects.ac.uk). National and local newspapers are a good source of job advertisements and many newspapers have a 'themed' day for specific sectors. In addition, you should explore trade and specialist publications. Many vacancies are now advertised online either on recruitment websites or on the employer's pages, so if you know which organisations are of particular interest you should check their websites regularly too. Other options include targeting specific businesses with speculative applications, investigating departmental data on the destinations of previous graduates and contacting both the employer and the graduate, and increasing your contacts through networking in the hope that you may learn of potential vacancies. In addition you may benefit from attending some of the larger events designed to introduce graduates and employers such as careers fairs, recruitment fairs and the 'milk round'.

The 'milk round' is the name given to the campus recruitment visits by employers. Traditionally it targeted undergraduates in their final year, with the jobs beginning the following autumn, but in recent years employers have also become interested in new graduates as well, and jobs and training schemes now commence at various times throughout the year. Organisations recruiting large numbers of graduates still tend to fill their vacancies at a particular time of year, mainly in the autumn, but smaller organisations recruit differently. As SMEs (small and medium sized enterprises with up to 250 staff) have become more important in terms of graduate recruitment, the annual milk round no longer dominates the recruitment calendar as SMEs seek to fill vacancies as and when they arise. For this reason it is a good idea to check sources for jobs regularly. The busiest time is predictably from May to September when undergraduates are looking past their finals to the future and employers realise that this is an opportunity to find talented individuals who have not previously been available for work.

Dealing with not knowing what you want

If at this late stage you still do not know what you want to do, it may be that you actually need to start a job in order to clarify what you particularly enjoy and what suits you. However, do not be tempted to apply for everything you see advertised since it is obviously beneficial to pick an area that is not too far removed from the choice you will eventually make. In order to narrow the scope to a manageable level you should work on ruling out those options that definitely do not appeal. Look at your skills audit and your list of personal attributes; make lists of what you enjoy and what you do not enjoy; read all job advertisements and try to account for your response to them; take personality and aptitude tests on line; and find out what previous graduates in your subject have gone on to do. You may also find it helpful to talk to share ideas with other graduates. Your university will be able to put you in touch with others in a similar position, and you can also talk online (www.prospects.ac.uk). If inspiration does not strike you during this process, then either select a large organisation where it may be possible for you to move internally once you have more knowledge of the options available, or look for work that is in some way connected with any hobby you may have. For example, if you enjoy travel, you might consider working for an airline or shipping company, or in the tourist industry; or if you like motorbikes, you might consider think about working at a key venue such as Silverstone, or for a bike magazine, manufacturer or sales outlet. Remember that all experience is good experience, but in the best case scenario it will be relevant to your next job.

▶ A positive outlook for jobhunting

If you have followed the guidelines offered in this book, you will by now be competent and practised in a wide variety of areas. These include reflecting on what you really want in terms of work and knowing where to find out about suitable opportunities; writing letters of application; adapting your CV to suit specific vacancies; coping with interview questions and protocol; using your current skills and developing new ones in a workplace environment; integrating with colleagues in the workplace; dealing with problems; understanding and appreciating perspectives other than your own; and expressing your observations and conclusions verbally and in writing in an articulate and perceptive manner. This is an impressive list of skills and one that will stand you in good stead as you embark upon your chosen career. Indeed, seeking, securing and undertaking a work placement parallels the quest to find and take on employment, albeit on a smaller scale, so you are now well-equipped and competent to tackle the job market.

At this point, therefore, the key points to keep in mind centre on your attitude. It is very important to be patient, as the best opportunity may not come along immediately. Try to remain enthusiastic and confident, as with continued effort and time you will be rewarded. Remember that self-reflection is a life-long learning skill, so use it to your advantage now and throughout your career by constantly examining and reappraising your own situation and any consequent action that is required. This may be particularly useful if you do pursue a route that you later decide is not the best one for you. Finally, be proud of your achievements, be aware of your ambitions, and be confident that you can identify and develop potential opportunities along your career path.

▶ Securing a job

As I have noted, finding a job is just one step further than finding a work placement so you should feel confident in your ability to deal with what lies ahead. However, you may find that the application process this time is more stringent and formal. You need to be prepared to send photocopies of your qualifications if requested; to give information about your health, and also to offer the names of both academic and personal referees. As references are very important, it is essential that you keep your referees updated as to your plans, and in particular that you send them copies of the job advertisement and person specification, together with your application, for any jobs for which they are expected to supply a reference. Each application is different and your referees may wish to tailor their response accordingly.

In some cases you may also be expected to take aptitude and personality tests, designed to ensure that you are the right person for the job in question. Aptitude tests are designed to measure intellectual capabilities for thinking, reasoning, analysis and logic. They may take the form of verbal or numerical reasoning multiple choice questions and are usually timed. Personality tests match attitudes and outlook to the job in question and sometimes the workplace. Occasionally the profile is compared to those of other staff in the section in order to attempt a compatible match, or alternatively, to introduce new perspectives into the group. Tests may take the form of multiple choice questionnaires, but if you are interviewed and asked about your interests, motivation and so on, be aware that your body language will also be observed. Several websites specialising in finding employment, for example www.prospects.ac.uk offer individuals the opportunity for self-testing aptitude and personality and it is wise to take advantage of this resource as it demystifies the procedure.

Some employers are also adopting the current vogue of unusual assessment methods, such as asking the candidate to think of themselves in terms of an animal and then explain their choice, or to draw a picture or even play a musical instrument for which they have not had lessons.[8] Clearly, if you do not feel comfortable with what you are asked to do you may choose not to work for an organisation that employs such recruitment methods. However, it may be in your interest simply to play along. The test may be designed to evaluate your initiative, your qualities as a team player or your ability for self-assessment. And you never know, you could reveal an aspect of your personality that is just what the employer is looking for!

▶ Receiving a firm offer

Whilst your offer of a work placement may have been very informal, a job offer together with an acceptance letter form a contract of employment

---

[8] See, for example, 'If you want to land this job, tell me what kind of a fish you are', in *Daily Mail*, 11 November 2003.

between you and your employer which is, as such, a legal undertaking on both sides. Once you have accepted a job offer, you are committed to starting work and not free to accept a subsequent offer from elsewhere. If you decide to accept, check that all the details in the letter are correct, such as the job title, the salary, the starting date and any references to, for example, pension rights. You should reply in full, referring to the date of the offer letter and quoting the job title given. If you accept the job, take the opportunity to thank the person concerned for the offer and express your enthusiasm for starting work with them. If you decide to turn the offer down, you should nevertheless send a polite letter thanking them for their interest. You never know when you may need to contact them again! In either event, try to reply promptly. It is important to keep all correspondence, but essential that you keep anything related to the job that you accept, in case any misunderstandings do arise later.

► Alternative courses of action

Setting up your own business/self-employment

Self-employment or setting up your own business is by no means an easy option, although for some people the benefits outweigh the problems. For many, the key benefit is the freedom associated with being your own boss. It is down to you how long you spend working, and on which projects. This can be particularly beneficial for those with personal commitments for whom flexible working arrangements are essential. If you have original ideas that you wish to develop and market, doing so through your own business may be the best option. Similarly, for those who have been made redundant and cannot break back into the sector or those who cannot find an opening in the first place, it may be sensible to try to gain a foothold by setting up a related business. In the case of new contributors to the workforce, this may well provide relevant experience that can be used in the future to approach employers within the sector. Some people leave their employers in order to set up on their own, as they prefer the experience of a smaller set-up in which they have more control, or they wish to offer a smaller, more specialised service.

However, there are many drawbacks to working for yourself, most particularly that work may be irregular and insecure. You may find yourself with too much or too little to do, resulting in working round the clock one month and being without work the next. Moreover, not knowing when or from where the next contract will come may be stressful and disconcerting. It is also likely that you will encounter cash flow problems, not just due to an irregular flow of work, but also because you may not be paid as promptly as if you were in a conventional job. In addition, you need to make your own pension and sick pay arrangements. It may also be much more difficult to differentiate between work time and personal time and you may discover that it is difficult to balance home and work commitments and that one or other of them suffers.

If you are considering self-employment or starting your own business, you need to be sure that you have the necessary motivation, self-reliance and commitment, and that you have the psychological make-up to cope with the potential insecurities and financial stresses and the realities of working on your own or with one or two others for large periods of time. You also need to ensure that there is sufficient demand for the products or services you intend to offer and that you have the necessary skills. You need to know where to find relevant business, financial and legal information and how to go about attracting outside finance if required.

There are abundant sources of information about setting up your own business, including your local Citizens Advice Bureau, Enterprise Agency, Job Centre and your university jobshop. You can find out about the financial aspects involved from free leaflets that are offered by several high street banks. Many organisations also provide free self-help guides or have sections of their websites devoted to 'frequently asked questions' and are thus a good place to start. Useful contacts include Companies House, the official government register of UK companies which issues several free guides (www.companieshouse.gov.uk); Lawyers for your Business, which offers a free consultation to discuss your business legal issues under the auspices of The Law Society (www.lfyb.lawsoc.org.uk); Better Business, a subscription magazine with a comprehensive FAQ section on its website (www.better-business.co.uk); and the Prince's Trust, a charity offering assistance and support to 18–30s who may encounter disadvantages in setting up their businesses (www.princes-trust.org.uk). You may also consider membership of one of the many organisations offering advice and support to its members on business matters, such as the Federation of Small Businesses (www.fsb.org.uk), which describes itself as *the* voice of small businesses, or your local branch of the British Chambers of Commerce (www.chambersonline. co.uk), or the CMI, Chartered Management Institute (www.managers. org.uk) which supports the development of professional management.

Further study

For some graduates, the option of further study is appealing. However, this is not necessarily an easy route and it is important that anyone considering it questions not only their motivation, but their ability to cope with the level and scope of the work, the lifestyle conditions imposed by further study and the effect on career options. It is undeniably expensive, not only because course fees and living expenses need to be covered, but also in the sense that it delays eventual entry to the job market. Moreover, whereas undergraduates tend to share similar circumstances, postgraduates and others engaged in further study are not so insular, as others of a similar age within their circles will be earning and leading a completely different lifestyle. The nature of the learning may also be different, as the student may at this stage be left more to his or her own devices. Moreover, the work may be difficult and focused, so it is essential to have selected an appropriate subject.

There are good and bad reasons underpinning decisions to opt for further study. If it is a requirement for career progression and advancement, as it can be in professions such as teaching, law and librarianship, it represents an extremely attractive option, as it will benefit the individual concerned in the long term. Indeed, in some instances, failure to achieve the relevant qualification will hinder career advancement. However, the situation is not always so clear cut. If you have enjoyed your subject at undergraduate level and are motivated strongly to explore it in greater depth, you may well find this a very satisfying course of action. This is sufficient reason in itself, but although it is not necessarily obligatory that the qualification will help in terms of a future career, it is essential to consider whether or not the usefulness of the qualification is a factor in the decision to proceed. Some students are under the impression that future employers will find additional qualifications attractive as they imply that the candidate has something special to offer. However, this is only likely to be the case if it is relevant to the job application in question. The converse may otherwise be true, as an employer may have concerns that the candidate's proven interests do not seem to support the application and imply that his or her real interests lie in another direction. The employer may therefore be reluctant to take on someone whom they feel may not stay in the company or may not be comfortable in that area.

Another 'good' reason for undertaking further study is to convert to a different area. You may, for example, have formed your career preferences towards the end of your undergraduate course which may not be as relevant to your chosen path as you would wish. A further year of study can remedy this by providing a relevant qualification, and, more importantly, proof of commitment to the new subject.

Probably the worst reason for opting for further study is to buy time before having to make a career decision. If you have not decided by the end of your undergraduate course, further study is unlikely to provide inspiration. Also, this rationale is unlikely to provide the motivation required to be committed to the subject and you may not find this course of action satisfying.

If you do wish to study further, it is very important to consider the various options. Academic postgraduate study is one avenue; another is professional training. You need to consider whether you would prefer to study full or part time and what you hope to achieve. You may also find that some employers are prepared to offer in-house training or offer financial support for a vocational training course.

Vocational training courses

If you want to update your skills formally with support and guidance from teaching staff whilst simultaneously undertaking paid employment, a vocational training course could represent the perfect combination for you. Although this option requires a high degree of self-motivation and hard work, participants are able to enjoy the benefits of working and studying and as such may be said to get the best of both worlds. The financial pressures of part-time study are likely to be far less than those of full-time study, especially if the person concerned is on a regular income. Moreover, in many cases the employer may be willing to contribute towards or even to cover the tuition fees and to give paid time off for attending the course and/or completing any necessary assignments.

Vocational training courses add value to the individual's CV as they prove that the person concerned has undergone recent professional development including an updating of skills and sector knowledge. They are indicative of a commitment to the work concerned and also imply a sense of focus and a willingness to work hard. In today's competitive job market this enhances employability. Combining study and paid work also means that it is possible to relate each to the other in a beneficial way. Not only will reflective skills improve, but also, work practices may be honed as a result of reflection so that they become more efficient, and developments in the workplace are also likely to be incorporated into the taught aspects of the course. Attending relevant conferences also offers opportunities for sharing information and networking, and research findings stand to benefit the sector generally. Although it is clearly necessary to set aside time to study whilst at home, there is normally a degree of flexibility involved and an organised person can usually work and attend a vocational course without too much encroachment on personal life.

▶ Summary

This chapter emphasised the importance of self-reflection after a work placement experience in order to identify and deal with any gaps in knowledge or skills. It then focused on how to create a jobsearch strategy with the aim of finding employment after graduation. This involved keeping track of sources of vacancies and the job market in general; updating the CV and skills audit; and reaffirming exactly what was being sought and why. It also offered suggestions for students unsure of their career preferences; those who wished to become self-employed and those interested in further study. Overall it argued that students who had followed all the guidelines in this book were well-equipped to tackle the process of finding and securing work, and that they should proceed with confidence, enthusiasm and patience.

Perspectives and Feedback

After working at xxx I feel that the charity sector is definitely a possibility for me as a career path. However, I think I would need to spend more time getting work experience with different types of charities to help me decide what aspect of a charity organisation most interests me. It would also be useful for me to see the way that other charities are run, especially the larger ones. It has definitely inspired me to pursue this line and try to get a job in the charity sector when I leave university.

Katrina, *student*

A lot of students used our placement positions so that they could bulk out their CV a bit and have a referee other than their college tutor. One placement student did end up as an employee, so it can be a good recruiting ground. Where else can an employee trial a student for a month or two before offering them a job!

Alistair, *employer – marketing for new media*

I worked in all areas of the bank and I particularly enjoyed working with customers at the customer service room and at the cashier desk. I was welcomed by all of the team there and was given treatment that I did not anticipate, for example they often took me out for lunch and I was given £x at the end for my hard work. What did surprise me was the fact that they allowed me to go down to the safe. It was a huge iron vault and the money was individually packed into separate safes. On another instance, I was given £5,000 to count using the machine. However, to my horror the machine whipped up the money and scattered it across the entire room. This was on my first day and I was still quite nervous. However, the staff laughed and helped me collect it up. After this experience I was very impressed with the way that they managed to balance having fun and enjoying their work with the tough work lives that they endured. I would definitely consider pursuing some work in this field.

Sandy, *student*

I am at the end of my experience and am still so far undecided about which career route to take and where I will finally end up. Museums are still an option but I have learnt through my experience that in order to succeed in the museum sector you have to be absolutely sure before beginning this career path and I feel personally that I want to explore further a few more avenues before I decide for certain.

Sophie, *student*

Placements don't guarantee a job. However, look for the transferable skills acquired during the placement. You may not necessarily find your dream job immediately but could use the experience in another field.

Sally, *employer – museum*

I think work experience is a fantastic idea. Even if it helps you decide what you *don't* want to do for a career, it is still an important experience, and gives you an interesting insight into other people's chosen careers.

Cathy, *student*

I think that work experience will be very useful to me: it is essential in applying to study medicine at university and will hopefully help me to decide whether medicine is the right career for me.

Valerie, *student*

I am focused on a career in Public Relations, which is a very competitive industry. The reason I chose to study at xxx university was entirely due to the work placement scheme. Very few courses incorporate two six month placements, which is a shame as it gives one an edge on other post graduates going in to the job market. My position at the Hospice was 'Communications Co-ordinator'. Unlike some placements I was hired to fulfil an essential role by co-ordinating several events, whilst also raising the charity's profile in other ways such as press releases, talks and newsletters. This constant variety enabled me to experiment creatively, develop my organisational skills and work under the pressure of constant deadlines.

Fiona, *student*

Having coped with such a large-scale [theatrical] production I feel, after I graduate, I can be confident enough to apply for jobs in arts administration, arts management, as a project worker or some type of community worker. I would find it rewarding and very challenging.

Mutiat, *student*

The process I went through at xxx has been helpful in guiding me in my future career. I was in a position to learn about other employees' work as well as my own placement. The whole experience has been eye opening for me. I think that it was a really important thing to have done before I graduate because I now have an idea of how the working world runs. It has helped me to work out what sort of career I would like once I have left university. Having the work experience on my CV will allow me to get into the industry and get a job more easily than if I only had my degree. I have made contacts that will prove invaluable in helping me find a job. I feel the work placement scheme is a great idea in helping final year students find their feet in the industry that appeals to them.

Anastasia, *student*

Appendix 1:
Employability Skills Sought by Employers

Skills sought by employers will vary according to the vacancy. However, general employability skills include the following:

Intellectual skills
- Numeracy
- Problem-solving abilities
- Evaluative and analytical skills
- IT skills
- Ability to relate theory to practice

Communication skills
- Good telephone technique and oral skills
- Ability to listen
- Written communicative skills
- Teamworking – participation without domination
- Managing relationships

Personal qualities and attributes
- Initiative
- Commitment to working hard
- Creativity
- Common sense
- Self-motivation and self-reliance
- Flexibility
- Organisational ability
- Enthusiasm

Attributes relating to personal conduct
- Personal presentation
- Punctuality
- Time management
- Pleasant demeanour

Appendix 2:
An Employers' Guide to Making the Most of the Student

Initial thoughts and actions

- Take time to consider how best a student could contribute to your organisation and compile a list of potential tasks to include individual and team projects, backlogs to be cleared, and so on. Try to ensure that there is plenty of variety in the list and that it includes work that will enable the student to use his or her initiative and take personal pride in the outcome.
- Identify the key skills you would ideally like the student to possess, together with any specific personal qualities.
- Decide upon where the student will work, to whom (s)he will report, the hours and timetable involved, whether or not s(he) will be paid and whether or not expenses will be reimbursed.
- Verify that the student is covered by your insurance policy.
- Put these thoughts into writing and send a copy to the university work placement tutor as this will help to guard against misunderstandings. Ask for details of the placement to be circulated amongst the students or posted on a notice board to ensure that all potential candidates are aware of the opportunity you are offering.
- Check that you are aware of, and can accommodate, the university requirements underpinning the placement. (This may, for example, mean organising the timetable to enable the student to have some free time to gather information about your company whilst on site.)

Meeting students

- It is in your interest to interview more than one candidate and, if possible, to see all applicants in a block.
- You may wish to ask candidates to bring a sample of their work to the interview.
- If possible, include the person who will be supervising the student in the interview process.
- Reiterate your expectations in terms of the work to be done and the terms and conditions in case there are unforeseen timetabling or other problems.
- When you appoint a candidate, send written confirmation of the terms and conditions, together with your expectations, as this will guard against misunderstandings.

At the start of the placement

▶ Set aside a time for an uninterrupted induction. The time for this will vary according to the nature of the work placement but it should include a tour of the premises, introductions to key personnel, an explanation of the health and safety procedures and an outline of the work to be done. This is also a good opportunity to ascertain that the student is absolutely clear about what is expected in terms of office etiquette – for example, the dress code, the times for starting and finishing work, arrangements for the lunch hour, and the policy about using the office telephone for personal calls.

▶ Make sure that the student knows to whom (s)he should turn in the event of dilemmas or problems.

▶ Make sure that you have details of a contact at the university to whom you can turn in the event of dilemmas or problems.

During the placement

▶ Give the student feedback at regular intervals and ask for his/her thoughts in return. Check that the student understands what is expected and is confident to proceed with the work.

▶ Try to arrange that if the student is engaged in menial work s(he) is not expected to do this all day. Variety will help to maintain the student's interest and enthusiasm.

▶ Introduce periods of 'shadowing' so that the student can get an overview of what others do and how the workforce interacts.

▶ Organise something for the student to do without supervision for times when his/her supervisor may be called away on other duties.

▶ Do give praise where it is deserved as your student may need confirmation that (s)he is on the right track!

After the placement

▶ Have a de-briefing meeting with the student as the feedback you receive may be useful to you for future occasions. If you wish, and particularly if you would like another work placement student from the same university, discuss the placement in detail with the placement tutor.

▶ Be prepared to be asked to supply a reference or to fill in some forms for the university.

Index

Work Experience

The **official magazine** of the
National Council for Work Experience
Published October 2004

Packed full of advice and information including:

- Placement vacancies for 2005
- Work experience factfile
- Why do work experience?
- Myths and truths about work experience
- International work experience
- Work experience for International students in the UK
- Case studies

To pick up your free copy, visit your university careers service or university job shop. Alternatively you can order direct from www.prospects.ac.uk/order

THE NATIONAL COUNCIL FOR WORK EXPERIENCE

work-experience.org

The National Council for Work Experience is a wholly owned subsidiary of Graduate Prospects and is dedicated to promoting, supporting and developing quality work experience for the benefit of students, organisations and the economy.

Visit **www.work-experience.org** for the most up to date work experience vacancies, case studies and latest news.